The People

The People

*The Sons of God
(Through the Eyes of a Watcher)*

Ian Heard

RESOURCE *Publications* · Eugene, Oregon

THE PEOPLE
The Sons of God (Through the Eyes of a Watcher)

Resource Publications
An Imprint of Wipf and Stock Publishers
199 W. 8th Ave., Suite 3
Eugene, OR 97401

www.wipfandstock.com

PAPERBACK ISBN: 978-1-5326-4828-1
HARDCOVER ISBN: 978-1-5326-4829-8
EBOOK ISBN: 978-1-5326-4830-4

Manufactured in the U.S.A.

Contents

Contents

Introduction

For behold, the darkness shall cover the earth,
*and deep darkness **the people** (ha am);*

But *the* LORD *will arise over you,*
and His glory will be seen upon you.

The Gentiles shall come to your light, and
kings to the brightness of your rising.

(Isaiah 60:2 NKJV **emphasis**
and parenthesis added)

JESUS THE MESSIAH SPOKE conclusively about two ways. Only two. Not a plethora of confusing options: a narrow gate onto a narrow way, leading to life, or, a wide gate onto a broad way leading to destruction. Yes, destruction. His unequivocal words crystallize the choice and describe the great divide within humankind—and within our history. At the same time, they also make the choice uncomplicated, attractive . . . and obvious! The history of our planet, in its simplest terms and as seen from God's perspective, entails the trajectories of these two paths to their respective destinations.

At the Fall in Eden, a shadow came into the heart of mankind and over the earth, which has ever since tried to engulf. Unless light had been offered and provided, darkness would have engulfed. Indeed, there have been times in earth's history when light has been all but snuffed out. Yet even at the darkest times there has remained a glimmer which has periodically shone brilliantly again, bringing all the change that only light can bring. The light that dispels the darkness has always been carried within, and by, people. God ordained it should be so; just as darkness entered through the heart of man, it pleased God that darkened mankind could be transformed—redeemed actually—to yet become bearers of light. The light originates with him—belongs to him; but those transformed by his light become light-bearers. In his word the light-bearers are known as both the benei ha Elohim—the sons of God—and, The People.

So, beyond the Fall two human streams emerged. One stream consisting of those who retrospectively understood God's statement through the incident with Cain and Abel and whose hearts remained predominantly like that of Abel. This stream of light and life flowed down through Adam's third son Seth (seen by Eve as Abel's replacement—see Genesis 4:25), then via Enoch, Lamech and Noah (see Genesis 5). The little sentence that concludes Genesis 4 is noteworthy and powerful; *at that time men began to call on the name of Yahweh.* This stream became recognized as the benei ha Elohim—sons of God. They are featured in Genesis 6 in what might be described as a 'second Fall' where a number of these benei ha Elohim became seduced by some beautiful daughters of those following the other stream—those now being known as the 'sons of men' (benei adam). These were those following the stream flowing spiritually in the same heart–attitude as Cain. Thus, the opening chapters of Genesis typify the entire post–Fall history of humankind, with its two trajectories and consequent cycles of darkness and light, darkness and light.

History is viewed properly only through the Biblical lens which provides the perspective from the throne-room of the One who created, sustains and governs it. Only the Bible provides the entire record of the contrasting trajectories of the two streams. It alone makes clear the ongoing call to, and choice for, all; to remain in a 'vagrant' land (the word used in Genesis 4:16) in the line of Cain as benei adam, or to come home and be re-united with our Creator in a redeemed and restored life as benei ha Elohim (as typified in Jesus' famous parable of the prodigal son).

The life of the sons of God is characterized by allegiance to and obedience to their Creator, in the person of Jesus Christ. This choice guarantees peace, assurance, identity and purpose. More importantly, it brings product that has everlasting consequence and value, by being joined with him in his work of new creation. It is the light-bearing life, intended to attract those among the sons of men who sense the yearning within, to come to the light. Life as a son of man is limited to human possibility at best—and to this life only. At worst it results in chaos, fragmentation and purpose-lessness. It is characterized by independence from God and exclusion from the grace and enabling that he offers for life sublimely different—and life which makes a difference, for eternity.

God's grace-filled purpose is to 'bring *many sons* to glory,'[1] He made it possible through an 'Elder Brother' who leads the way through the narrow gate and along the narrow path, as the new Representative Man; one made like us, in God's extraordinary plan to carry us with him across the yawning gulf from darkness to light. *The* Son of God became a new son of man, a new Adam, so that we, in him, may become sons of God.

This is history's grand plan and trajectory. Don't miss your part in it as one of those known as *the sons of God*.

1. Hebrews 2:10–11

Part One: **Why a people?**

Dear Human Reader:

I am one among those known as the Watchers; but one, among the hosts called by the name Eir. We are also called Qodesh (or Kaddesh)—the Holy Ones.[1] I have been known as Shaqaad, or to you who read, Wakeful. When your scriptures say that 'the eyes of Yahweh run to and fro throughout the earth'[2] it is, as it were, through us. We have been commissioned, for example, to be watchful for those among the humans whose hearts are wholly for him. We are from a realm where time as you experience it, does not exist—and yet, we can also move within your realm to perform commissions in time and upon your abode, which you call Earth. Since your beginning I have been assigned as a Watcher.

When I say that we are to be engaged particularly in behalf of those who are wholly for Yahweh, you must understand that since near your beginning there has been a division—indeed a gulf—between those so disposed to him that they will not be separated, and those who willfully choose paths of their own invention. We call those inclined to his heart the 'benei ha Elohim'—Sons of the Elohim as you can tell from the scriptures he has so carefully entrusted to you;[3] but more on this soon. As a Watcher, I have

1. Daniel 4:13, 17, 23 (NKJV)

2. 2 Chronicles 16:9 (NKJV)

3. Genesis 6:2 (NKJV). Note the many scriptures that use this imagery, e.g., Ex. 4:22–23; 2 Sam. 7:14; 1 Chron.17:13, 28:6; Job 1:6 and 2:1; 38:1–7; Jer. 31:20; Psalm 2:7; Hosea 1:10; Matt. 5:9; Luke 6:35, 20:34–36 (note here 'sons of this age and sons of God'; Romans 8:14; 2 Cor. 6:18 and etc. (all NKJV). Carefully note the Dead Sea scrolls reading of Deuteronomy 32:8 'when the Most High gave the nations their inheritance, when He separated the sons of man,

1

observed the diverging paths and have felt the pain that Yahweh knows.

I have been granted permission to set down in an earth language what we have observed, particularly as it relates to those who were called to a special purpose—that of providing a clear, visible picture of the high ground that leads to Yahweh's presence and life, protection and provision.

We too, are created beings—and are also benei ha Elohim, but of a different class and order, for we have been made by him for an altogether different purpose. But my hope is that you, human reader, will, inasmuch as is granted to your class of being, become not only a true son of Elohim, but also a wakeful and watchful one. Whatever has been entrusted to me by ha Elohim to assist in this, I must do.

For you,

In His Majesty's joyous thrall and service,

WATCHER SHAQAAD

He set the borders according to the number of the sons of God.'

CHAPTER 1

Responsibility

THE MAN, 'DAM, AND his wife Chaveh had known no disquiet, nor apprehension, nor alarm; only the deep-calm, replete-ness of shalom. Not that they would have described their condition as such, for having known nothing but this, there was no different experience for comparison. It would have been like trying to describe darkness where only light was known; like asking what emptiness means when nothing but fullness has been experienced. Or like asking what apprehension was (as a Watcher I have been permitted an inkling of your feelings and senses)—when confident assurance and its strength, flowed daily from them in their relationship with the created world. 'Dam and Chaveh communed with The Source straight from their inmost place. . . . sensed him as one near at hand with whom they shared a partnership in which they knew, innately, their role: to reproduce after their kind and to bring the place Edhen in which they dwelt (and beyond) to its utmost productivity and beauty as a perfect reflection of his desire. They sensed at once both the profundity and the immense joy of their commission; they walked as one with The Source! And the man and the woman communed with the other creatures too, with a kind of unspoken yet distinct understanding that flowed between them (as it flows in the world I inhabit), often without need for speech or sound. This inward knowing needed no explanations and prompted no questions: they were one with The Source and functioned simply as a flowing extension and local expression of his creativity and glory—in much the same way as I do!

It was altogether different to the reader's experience of the created world and therefore difficult to make real to twenty-first century men and women, for it was a place and a condition beyond your imagining. I can but attempt to help you understand. For a start, there was a union and a flow of events and creatures and things organic and inorganic that seemed to sing in the most glorious harmony, a song of praise and majesty; and to dance the most synchronized, joy-filled dance of joined movement and purpose. And the song and the dance comprised the mysteriously productive union in which each single thing as well as all things together, worked for the good of every other thing in a symphony of productivity! Nothing at all like the wearisome effort required in your day and time to effect anything lasting. Nothing was gripped by the thrall that is the bane of the reader's life, requiring greater and greater expenditure of energy to maintain things against decay and corruption, disease and death. None of that sense of struggle within a system pitted against productivity; those ever-limiting factors that work against, rather than for, fruitfulness.

Diminishing returns are the hallmark of effort in your day. But then! Why— everything contributed to the song and dance of creation; a vast choral and symphonic movement whose product was greater than the sum of its parts, yet in which no part was without profound significance to the product. It is written in your own annals that the morning stars sang and the benei ha Elohim shouted for joy![1] Oh yes, the joy! Why, there was nothing but happiness and the contentment of flourishing in everything to which the man and the woman put their hands. As we've said, it is beyond the limits of mind and vocabulary to properly describe with your kind of words on a page. I can but instruct and point your imagination dear reader, to its sublime, other-worldly nature. I say other-worldly, because your present experience of the world is a thing altogether removed from that. As you say—as chalk to cheese; as vinegar to wine. To your day and your experience, a vain

---

1. Job 38:4ff where the writer is speaking of an earth already formed but before the spoiling of the Fall

and fanciful wish. If only! But, my dear reader—that is how it was; in the beginning!

Yet, something occurred, yes, on one of those sublime days, that made heaven recoil. As I have said, the man and the woman were clearly the crowning glory of the entire fabric, yet with ability to commune with all the lesser creatures, over whom they had supervision simply for the joy of bringing all to fullness of purpose. I say that the other creatures were inferior because the man and woman were a crowning glory, being as they were, of an entirely different order of being. For Creator in his limitless wisdom had made all sorts and orders of beings—yet only one among all of them in the likeness of his own being! There is the class to which I belong; angelic seraphim and kheruvim and archangelic beings, all with roles outside of the time-bound sphere; huge hosts of them, equipped for the effecting of Creator's will and deeds in realms different to yours, as well as within yours! Commissioned to effect his will and bring worship, honor and glory to him in all things. Oh, it is quite outside the grasp of your minds now, especially in their current condition. And then there was Man, a little lower in rank than all of us, for his realm of responsibility was to be time-bound and limited within that realm. But his distinctive, setting him entirely apart from the angelic ones, was that he was uniquely like The Source; like Creator! Made in his image if you please! Like the Elohim One made material, within time—and to be in charge, in co-regency with him, of a material realm and all its creatures. Commissioned as proxy for him, to bring the newly-created time-world and its sub-worlds of creatures and vegetation to the full harmony of productivity; to be the conductor in that realm of the song, the dance, the symphony!

Two trees!

The Human creatures were of neutral disposition. Just as they knew no disquiet because there was nothing to cause it, so too, they had no inkling of a disposition other than goodness. To suggest that anything was deficient in the song or in the harmony and the dance, would have been ludicrous to them just as it would have been to suggest any possibility of a thing opposite the goodness and pleasure they experienced. And yet, that suggestion came; and it came from one of the creatures—or at least, through one of the creatures as mouthpiece. For the fact was that there were two voices—just as there were two significant trees whose purpose signaled Creator's desire to allow freedom of choice to his crowning glory.

The one tree represented life, light and flow and everything that things should *become*. It stood as a statement—indeed it exemplified, potential. It was a handsome tree, full of fruit and whose fruits offered new delights of taste and inspiration with every mouthful. 'Becoming' was the intention: all created things being sung and danced from a kind of neutrality into largesse of productivity. I say from neutrality because the direction in which creation moved—either to multiplication or diminution, progress or regress—was to depend on the choices made by this Elohim-like creature. And they were indeed the key. Such was the onus placed upon the man, 'Dam and the woman, Chaveh. This remarkable privilege was given because the desire of Creator was that the creature be as like to himself as was possible in the new realm. A reflection of him, having creative stewardship to nurture everything under their command to its majestic potential; a veritable viceroy god-creature! As I've said, an awesome privilege indeed.

And oh, how this creature was loved by Creator. Loved because he stood as proxy in the new world; loved because he was as like him as it was possible to be within a necessarily limited realm; loved because the intention in bringing him to life was just that—to be an object of love and to be loved in a partnership of creativity.

And yes, the other tree: it stood as representative of a world not to be entered upon, but of whose existence the creature was to be aware if he was to be in all respects like his Creator. It represented all that was contradictory, negative and subversive; a world of shadow. For how could light be fully appreciated unless darkness remained a constant possibility? How could fruitfulness have meaning unless barrenness also was possible? The creatures must know that there existed a world, a realm not to be visited, that was opposite to—indeed opposed to, theirs. They needed to know and be warned to ignore it and always to prefer life and joy, productivity and multiplication. They were also required to recognize that, even though they had enormous freedoms, they were freedoms within boundaries set by Creator for their good. Choice provided onus; it imposed responsibility. The new class of being could rise or fall at his own hand (as could some in my own order of being). And I saw as I watched that it was a risk Creator was willing to take so that their relationship could be of the level of mutuality he desired. The love of Creator for you, this new order of being was to be of the type that is built on trust between like beings.

And so, the future of your new realm was made to depend entirely upon your trustworthiness as its crowning creation. The stakes were high and therefore the temptation, cunning!

CHAPTER 2

Irresponsibility

I WATCHED AS THE greater light ascended over low hills in the east to send its golden greeting into leafy crowns and then to descend the trunks of a stand of gorgeous cedar and oak. The trees responded with a stirring in their giant limbs and a shiver in their leaves as a scented breeze, also aroused by the Sun, played around and through them. The lesser light was still high though translucent, in a bright western sky. Birds great and small called and preened and stretched wings. The springing streams that flowed out of Edhen to carry their life throughout the land could be heard, tinkling and gurgling. The great mist of the night was already ascending above tree-tops and would soon evaporate to become part and parcel with the canopy of blue above, as it did each day. The woman Chaveh also stirred. She had been in her husband's arms and gently eased herself away to greet the new day and commune with Elohim as well as with birds and animals. Her communication was mostly without sound—a kind of knowing what was within and radiating from, each one; and they too, knew her feelings and her desires for each of them. It was that kind of wordless communication that even in your distant day I have occasionally seen in a husband and wife who've walked together a long time; a vestige that you sense, just beyond reach, of how it ought to be. I say as a vestige because where it occurs, it serves as a tantalizing reminder of something lost. The glimpsing of it on occasion even causes some to seek its recovery, though often by foolish means. But it cannot return unless at the behest of The One who first gave it—when hearts re-connect to him by the only means he has provided. Truth is, it was not so much lost as forfeited.

And I saw that as Chaveh walked in that far-back place she was experiencing the self-same joys and delights every creature enjoyed—enjoying them, and with them in untrammeled mutuality, the life of Creator Elohim in their midst. As one, they were making the song —melody and harmony—and indeed, symphony and it ascended to Elohim who joined in the delight as I, Shaqaad the Watcher did also! His presence was tangible and communicable. Oh, it was, to your now distant view, beyond what is called natural; in fact, beyond comprehension (unless, as hinted at before, and by virtue of entry into what is now called New Creation, the reader has been touched with measures and tastes of restoration). I see that it is the stuff of the deepest-in desire of your now distant hearts to enjoy again—and is desperately sought by many means. But in the beginning, it was the normal condition. This is how things were in Edhen. What was not normal, was what occurred on the day of which I speak, as the woman, Chaveh walked, communing, overflowing, anticipating the day and its trajectory of bounty and satisfaction.

Invasion!

The one, Abaddon the Destroyer, Adversary, Beelzebub, Prince of Darkness (none of which names come near describing his malevolence) and who once was one of us in an exalted responsibility—out of the farthest, deepest recesses of his own separated gloom, arose upon that day within the time realm with an inglorious scheme. To incite Creator to hate his creation and, if possible, regret the glorious plan foreordained—and to which he, Lucifer, in his exalted position, had once been privy. Now he, both grotesquely contorted and consumed with his own rejection, overflowing with regret over lost privilege and wishing revenge on Creator, had become the antithesis of all he once was. The bearer of light had become the bearer of darkness! It was a pitiful and preposterous plan from a now pitiful being. It was all that he remained capable of in his withered state. Mind you, even this diminished state presented a supernatural being of significant and quite awesome power—albeit as supremely ugly as he was once supremely beautiful. He was (and is) jealousy and malevolence personified, whose scheme was to share his own eternal rejection with as many of these new human creatures as possible. It was exactly because 'Dam and Chaveh were the crown—and made responsible—that they were the target.

He began his attack (as he continues) by subterfuge (the only way he knows), somehow to present himself in the guise of one of your time-realm creatures, the better to present his case. Oh, it was subtle; for what possible lack could there be for the man and the woman who dwelt in sweet commune and productive partnership with The One who had brought them forth from soil and rib for sublime, eternal purpose? They were living for The Purpose, with no sense of need. Ah, but perhaps a sense of lack could be created, could it not, by the suggestion that something had been withheld? Abaddon too, I have seen, can be creative; but he in the craft of evil, for where there appears to be no way to spoil, he can, by guile and deception, make a way. It is a practised art, driven in his case by the utter, final and unmitigated contempt he harbors for the One to whom he owed his being; the One who will ultimately consign him to everlasting ignominy. In the meantime, he has strength and ability greater than Man, for he is of our higher order. He has power yet, to disguise himself as light in subtle counterfeit. His strength therefore is greater than that of man, but not greater than that of Man in partnership with Creator. Ah—and alas, I see that it is only a momentary stepping away by Man from such privileged partnership that permits this one his strength. And that is why such subtlety is employed; to entice you to step away; for it can take but a moment of neglect, of infatuated distraction, of lassitude, of comparison. And the deception remains the suggestion that the Elohim One might be holding out on you—indeed, is withholding something from you that really ought to be yours. I knew this as I watched, yet Yahweh Elohim would not allow my direct intervention. I sensed that this was an event in which I was not permitted to intrude. It was a sacred and determining moment between Elohim and the creature made in his image. Though I could not understand it, I knew I was not permitted any interference for something intended for the time realm and its future was being established. It was beyond the boundaries of my apprehension.

Dissonance

And so, Abaddon, through one of the well-recognized creatures whom 'Dam had named, asked of Chaveh, "has Elohim placed a prohibition on any of these trees in the garden?" (knowing full well that he had). The serpent creature, with whom Chaveh had often shared the song and the dance in Elohim's presence, took Chaveh by surprise! Previously all that had mattered was the joined harmony. This transfer seemed to enter her spirit as a slight dissonance which at first made her start. Something in the serpent's demeanor had altered. Questions had never been part of the song or the dance or the communing. All of life till now had been resounding affirmation of and to, the glory of the great Creator Elohim and of the developing partnership with him. Yet, into Chaveh's spirit this day came this new and alien thing, albeit from a familiar source. It was a question and she knew the answer.

"Yes—we may eat of all the trees, save one, the one in the middle of the garden. The man 'Dam says that Elohim instructed us never to eat of it—and 'Dam himself added that we should not even touch it, lest we be brought into dissonance with Elohim."

Chaveh was right. There is a realm that you knew not of and were not to know. I have seen it and I knew exactly why Elohim desired your protection from it. Its name is 'death'. "Ah", says the one who through his guise would entice her to join him in that realm of rejection and so bring pain to Elohim, "there's no way you'll experience the thing called death; what you will experience is something he is experiencing and yet withholds from you! For he knows that in eating, your eyes too will be opened and, like him you'll see that there is another side that is being kept from you. You'll see the difference. Believe me, I too know both sides and have I ceased to be? Look, how beautiful is the fruit?" And I saw that it was the fear of missing out, indeed of being shut out; of being un-included by Creator in a special matter that even a lesser creature knew—that the deceiver used to bring you undone. Chaveh experienced a new sense; the suggestion of something desirable, withheld from them, lodged within, followed by a new desire—to know what it could possibly be. It was the trick. Persuaded that she ought to know, she took hold; and ate. And took some to eat with the Man, who without questioning, ate also. And that was the moment—when 'Dam also ate and became a participator—that was the moment of entry into the other realm;[1] the moment of dissonance that reverberated throughout the entirety of the vast creation, as Abaddon gained the means to share his own rejection and dissolution with the prized Creature! I too shuddered. Now Creator Elohim would surely hate not Abaddon only, but also the Crowning Creature. What had been Lucifer's weakness became man's. He had shared his darkness and spoiled another creature.

What I witnessed in that moment, once both had succumbed to deceit, is almost beyond that which words on a page in any of your languages, can describe. For I knew where it could have—should have, been prevented. For the woman should never have listened to one of the creatures over whom they had been given dominion; and then . . . the man should never have completed the act. He could have and should have governed and said no.

I perceived that had he done so, the terrible consequence that ensued would even yet have been prevented. Instead, the whiteness and the separateness, the pristine innocence and joy within which the Elohim One walked and communed with what he had created, instantaneously became jaundiced and put into a state of non-alignment. Every living creature within the blink of an eye, moved from joyful other-centered-ness to furtive and protective self-consciousness and self-centeredness. Even the inanimate objects lost their shine and hue, so that they at once appeared less alive and lacking in radiance. Whether this was because the Creature's eyes lost their ability to see innate glory, or it was a loss of

---

1. Genesis 3:7 *'then* the eyes of *both* of them were opened . . . '

glory in each object—or indeed a combination of both, is beyond me to discern. But I could see it too! Lackluster it all became; I saw it happen, and the Creature knew why and hid in shame and sudden remorse amidst bewilderment and urgent thoughts of how it could be retrieved. Oh, tragic does not come near describing the event and the outcome. The spoiling seemed to resound around the entire created realm as in vain 'Dam and Chaveh looked near and far for a trace of how it had been. Even the great hosts of created lights in the heavens lacked luster and resonance. And too, the Creature realized, with a hence unexperienced pang at deep-in level, that the communing had evaporated and the lesser creatures looked at them now with alarm and suspicion . . . . and fled away! Nothing remained the same; I saw that to them, fruit tasted different and alien plants began to spring up and choke fruitful trees. Some of their favorite trees suddenly knew disease and the thing called death. Even the grasses that had adorned the ground seemed forlorn and opaque where once vibrant and almost transparent. A pervading sense of 'less-ness' now defined their realm and their existence as a great and indescribable pall overhung, spoiling every waking moment.

The song too, had ceased; that sense of cooperative adventure with The Elohim, with all things blending together in verdant pleasure—where was it? WHERE WAS IT? Indeed, the silent shout from the depths of 'Dam and Chaveh was, "WHERE IS IT?" in an agony of that other thing they'd never known and I had only seen displayed in Lucifer—regret! For in their hearts they knew; and the answer came in upon them like a weight too heavy to be borne.

Crushing; inescapable; unrelenting. Sleep fled away, and Night, once beautiful in such a different way to Day, became a hated terror that never seemed to end, and when it did, gave way to yet another forlorn and grief-filled day. And the awful truth was that a new regime had been ushered in; and the Creatures knew they were responsible and became full of pangs never felt before—and when Elohim came calling, they shrank away. Oh, the one, Abaddon, had been correct indeed! For here in truth were new things not meant for their eyes, but they did not enjoy the seeing of them. Now they saw—and compared the less-ness with the wholeness and the contrast dogged their thoughts; the shadowy with the clear; the evil with the good and, the absence with the Presence. They knew shame and uncovered-ness. And, they were aware of new things between them both; blame and fault-finding and deception. And yet; and yet, despite the irresponsibility, I saw that Elohim tended them with love-care and forbearance. He felt their pain and covered their shame, but nevertheless had to cut off access to that other vital tree, lest the possibility through it, of immortality, should lead to the unhindered growth of self-will. A hedge was placed around the possibility of an exponential explosion of corruption. Death would henceforth circumscribe runaway darkness. They were expelled from the spoiled Edhen and I was instructed to place a kheruvim messenger with what they saw as a flaming and flashing weapon to prevent re-entry to that once wonderful place of the Presence.

To the reader, I, Shaqaad, have this to say: in your day and for you also, there are two trees, for the Tree of Life has been restored. We will have more to say on this at a later time; but the Tree has, as promised, arisen from the Root of Jesse[2] and you, like 'Dam and Chaveh must be careful, lest in trying to draw your sustenance from the tree of knowledge, you miss the Tree of Life!

(And what of the heart of the One, the Elohim who had created you, the extraordinary creature, as a reflection of Himself? It was of his Spirit that he created you and made you live. That Spirit was to 'light' everyone born as human[3] and over that light he yearned and yearns with envy[4] until it be returned by choice to the One who gave it!)

2. Isaiah 11:1ff & Romans 15:12
3. John 1:9
4. James 4:5

CHAPTER 3

Possibility: emerging streams; sons of God & sons of men

AND SO, I OBSERVED in time that from the now vitiated humans emerged two distinct streams as they bore children. One stream flowed from hearts that responded affirmatively to a consciousness they found arising within. For since *that* tree, it seemed that each found within, a sense of either 'I ought' or 'I ought not' which surfaced most strongly when deciding, for example, about responses and attitudes to others. The 'I ought' was related to things light, bright, self-effacing and of benefit to others; the contrasting sense of, 'I ought not' to things and actions now discernible as shadowy, grey or somehow dubious. Where good had been the only possibility (as it is in the realm that I inhabit) now this new thing, difficult for me to comprehend—the possibility of choosing something other than good, something in a shadowy realm away from light, had become for them, an introduced constant. Its presence was demonstrated no more clearly than with the men Qayin and Havel, sons of 'Dam. For, as your ancient record discloses, they each responded differently to inner promptings that called forth a response to Creator, the great Other to whom they knew they owed their existence. And I saw that one, the one named Qayin, responded with an offering of the fruit of the ground, the other with an offering of the firstborn of flock and its fat portions.[1] Havel, I saw, was discerning and selective, bringing as his act of devotion the first and the best and I could see in his motive a desire to draw

1. Genesis 4:4

near and to please. I have understood that such a heart in you humans does indeed please Elohim[2]—it is the constant disposition of those of my order of being. I have observed in your case, that it has to do with the kind of friendship Elohim One desires that you have with him, and I have learned its name! Its name is Faith or Belief, and I have come to see it as the foundation, not only for rejoining him, but also for an eventual redemption for you of things lost from Edhen. Qayin, as far as I could discern his motive, had not the same thing in his heart, thus treating Creator with disdain as though he would be satisfied with a token.

Creator made it clear to both that one was acceptable, the other, not—whilst at the same time making the most merciful and tender overture to Qayin who had become enraged.

"Qayin," said Yahweh into his inner being, "if you do what is pleasing, will not your offering, and you, be dignified with my acceptance? But Qayin, if your choice is to do what is not pleasing be aware that at your door is a crouching beast named chatta'ah (known as sin in the reader's language) with an appetite for you and you must master it or it will devour you."[3] It was, as you will see, even as I did, that Elohim yearns for a heart that desires to please him so that he can meet it with the dignity of acceptance. These are things mysterious to us, but as I watch, I get an inkling of their meaning; both to him and to you!

The twin dignities of purpose and acceptance were what Qayin craved, yet to receive it required a step back; an ownership of the thing in his heart that had come up short and therefore, displeased; a relinquishing of wrong attitude, a humility. Instead, he allowed resentment to fester. The thing called sin had been but crouching, ready, but Qayin had no desire to master it. He enjoyed and cultivated the anger and desired to exact revenge over his brother's acceptance and he shut out Yahweh's voice; and made his own plan—and so the thing that had been crouching sprang and

2. Hebrews 11:4; the difference is clearly defined here as faith, the disposition that pleases God

3. Genesis 4:6,7 where the imagery is of a crouching beast lying in wait just outside.

overpowered him. Oh, I watched it occur and yet it remained outside my command to prevent. Qayin murdered Havel! Took away the thing that only Elohim can give! It made me recoil and wonder what would happen. The thing called death had truly entered. Yet as always, Creator came near and Qayin was deceitful and punishment came and he went away from the presence of Yahweh to wander in lost-ness and grief in a land known in your language as Vagrancy.[4]

Divergence

I watched as the two streams diverged further and flowed away from each other in different directions, not unlike your great water streams that flowed from Ghan Edhen with ever-widening separation and distinctives. The stream from those who responded as Qayin had, flowed into a wilderness of alienation and insecurity. Even so, Creator in His unconquerable kindness promised to take care of Qayin. But the other stream! It became the stream of acceptance and purpose and security.

So, you see, the brothers Havel and Qayin typify the separation that exists down to your own day between those who, by what Creator defined as faith, have pleased him and become accepted, and those who neither believe nor heed his voice (whether whispered or raised).

It was, as your ancient record says, in the days of Seth, (the third son of 'Dam)—and his son Enos, that men began to call on the name of Yahweh![5] The stream from Seth then flowed through fathers like Henoch, who walked with and revered Yahweh Elohim and was taken without the thing called death. The other stream flowed from those who chose to walk only after newly-awakened, fleshly arousals. It became the stream of self-gratification, creating an ever-increasing distance between themselves and the Elohim of Henoch. And, as the streams flowed in their separate courses, I

4. Genesis 4:16 Hebrew NOD or NOWD means vagrancy
5. Genesis 4:26

perceived that the difference as well as the distance between them became the more noticeable. For one stream was accompanied by productivity and shalom, a clear life-giving flow, whilst the other (at least to my outside observation) seemed always to be accompanied by contention and loss. Those in that stream sank into corrupt, self-serving and indeed, self-defeating ways for it flowed into an unproductive, stagnant morass. It was not a stream of 'living water'. As I have said, the difference was observable and resulted in those in the latter stream becoming spiteful toward those within the clear, bright stream—just as I had seen Qayin become spiteful toward Havel. Those of the one stream began to be called *benei ha Elohim*, sons of God; the other, flowing as it sadly did, away from him, produced those known as *benei adam*—sons of men.[6] It was from them, as your scriptures say, that the tower at Bavel, came.[7]

6. Re sons of God and sons of men.
Benei ha Elohim (sons of God) is used in at least five places in our O.T. It also features significantly in the New (in its Greek form). We should consider the term in both testaments as consistent. Its use in the New picks up on its use in the Old to provide continuity. Genesis 6:1–4, Job 1:6, 2:1 and 38:7, in the Author's view, refer not to angelic beings but to those who have inclined their hearts toward God. In the New Testament, we see 'sons of God' (huioi theou) in passages such as Matthew 5:9; Luke 20:36; John 1:12; Romans 8:14, 19; Galatians 3:26; Ephesians 2:16; Philippians 2:15; 1 John 3:1.
Benei adam (sons of men) see e.g., Psalm 11:4; 33:13–14; 45:2; 57:4; 115:16; Proverbs 8:4; Ecclesiastes 3:18; Micah 5:7; Mark 3:28; Ephesians 3:5. Of Egypt's fall, Ezekiel said that they would all go down to the pit with the *benei adam*—the sons of men (Ezekiel 31:14). Psalm 53:2–3 says, 'God has looked down from heaven upon the *benei adam* to see if there is anyone who understands, who seeks after God. Every one of them has turned aside; together they have become corrupt; There is no one who does good, not even one' (See also Psalm, 33:13). God is forever looking for those among the *benei adam* who will incline their hearts to him!
7. Genesis 11:5 NKJV. Note, 'the LORD came down to see the city and tower which the *benei adam* had built.'

CHAPTER 4

Upheaval

I, SHAQAAD BEHELD, THAT the further the streams flowed through what you call time, the less alike they were. What I have called the streams were represented by the thing I had seen in the heart of Havel contrasted with the thing I had seen in Qayin. One, of that thing you and the scriptures Yahweh has provided you, called faith; the other, its opposite, I suppose nonfaith or unfaith, or perhaps just indifference! But what was in their hearts has continued flowing out and each tends to reproduce after its kind; faith begetting faith, un-faith begetting indifference until I wondered what Yahweh Elohim would do. I knew he would not be pleased, for your humankind was also rapidly multiplying in the Earth and what I beheld in fact, was that the stream that looked like Qayin's heart not only grew wider and fuller but the other stream—the Havel stream grew narrower! So wide did the Qayin stream become that at certain seasons and places it overflowed the Havel stream!

"Oh—what is to be done? What will the Elohim One, our Yahweh do?" The question had some urgency as it issued from the lips of the youthful Shem to the attention of his father, a robust, forceful and resourceful man whose name was Nuach. He had been named thus because his father, Lamech, had reflected on the desire in people's hearts in those days. That farthest-in desire was indeed nuach (or relief as it is called in the reader's tongue) and Lamech had said prophetically over his firstborn son, "for he will bring relief from the anxious toil caused by the cursed ground."[1] And now Nuach's firstborn, Shem (meaning Renown, because his father desired that by following Elohim, he would be made great), was perplexed.

You, dear reader must begin to see as I do, that the men speaking above are of those who followed the stream that flowed through Seth from the same heart as Havel. In your scriptures, those who set down the annals had begun to call them, appropriately you will agree, benei ha Elohim (sons of God).

One of the benei ha Elohim, that noble and upright man Nuach, had been telling Shem the story of the beginnings and Shem was curious about how things were then; and how they had come to be as they now were, in his day.

Shem, and indeed each of the man's three sons, had hearts like that of their father; hearts to seek the pleasure of Elohim. Shem had observed things that offended his soft heart; offended the Elohim-Presence within him. Appalling things like men hating, killing and maiming and performing offensive acts between them and with children and with animals; men robbing and plundering or deceitfully acquiring the product of others. It made his heart squirm; it was so misaligned with what his deep-heart said was right and productive. All that he had come to know of the Elohim One was brightness, light and certainty, but closing around him and family was a contrasting, repugnant darkness. True, life was not always easy with its constant struggle against a cosmos that seemed intransigent against efforts to make it productive, but Shem had already seen a principle at work; the more he sought cooperation with Creator and the more he kept his heart single as Father Nuach had taught him, the more unexpected surprises arrived with timely productivity and even surplus. He gave thanks to Yahweh, for he knew the goodness and blessing came from him.

"It is how Creator meant it to be" Father Nuach would say as Shem and the younger sons Cham and Yefeth marveled when they saw this occur.

1. Genesis 5:29

20

Yefeth, whose name in your tongue is Enlargement, could see the connection between the name his father had given him and the events of their lives. And it stood in stark contrast to what they observed everywhere around them among those now known as benei adam.

"Yes" continued Nuach, my father and grandfather taught me that the beginning was lightness and brightness and bounty; a joyful knowledge of bringing creation to fullness together with the Elohim One. The place where they lived was Edhen, full of fruitful growth where all creation joined in pure song-like cooperation that brought praise to him. They say that it was all good and right and clean—no badness, no decay, no death—and a tree that gave life. Nor any self-centeredness or competition. Can you imagine such a thing when now all that we see is impurity and a seeking after self?"

The Drift

With sad eyes looking out over a hillside mottled with moving shadows as a westering sun tried to see through wind-blown myrtle and acacia, the man continued, "there is a thing that occurs against which we must always guard."

"And that is?" queried Cham.

"There is, what shall I call it? The drift. . ." Nuach paused and the boys anticipated as he pondered and chose his words carefully, "It is incremental and it is subtle. It occurs whenever we suppress the desire for brightness that remains within our hearts; when we think we can produce it for ourselves. If we do not guard in our hearts what he has shown and taught, and forget that he is altogether different and, and . . . . other, yes, that's the word; he is altogether apart from inclinations that have invaded and find residence inside us and which we might so easily choose. I am thankful that he has given me a sense, ever since I set my heart to walk with him as father Henoch and my own father Lamech did, of this other-ness that distinguishes him. I know, as I have taught you, my sons, how offended he is when we forgetfully follow darker, resident inclinations. His desire is for us to walk with him in the place he walks, indeed, in a similar kind of other-ness from the darkness. It's a matter of choosing the brightness." The father smiled as the thought of it brought peace and pleasure to his whole being that manifested in a brightness in his own countenance and smile. (I, The Watcher felt pleasure too and I knew why this man had found favor in Yahweh's eyes!)

Nuach's deep-brown eyes smiled too, with a sparkle and gaze that communicated what his heart knew. It was the product of well-practised choices.

"I'm not sure I follow you, Father" broke in Yefeth. "You speak of this drift and this, what did you call it? Other-ness? Can you explain it differently?"

"Yes" says the wise, ageing man, "I think my thoughts are becoming clearer. The word I used was the best I could find. He is Creator and therefore what he has made stands away and separate from him but is to look like a work of his; to bear his mark and even his image and likeness—unmistakably his." The father reminded his attentive sons of how it was with things that they had crafted, such as farming implements and tools and tents. They stood as separate items from them and yet often mysteriously reflected their character and nature so that an observer could say, "that was made by Yefeth and this by Cham." Nuach reminded them that that's how it is with Creator Yahweh, but now in a different way to then. Whereas it all once perfectly represented him, it is now a spoiled representation. He told them that it's as though someone had taken a beautiful bow made by Cham—recognizable as his work—and then twisted or distorted it so that it was no longer properly fit for its purpose; its distinctiveness and effectiveness ruined so that arrows shot from it always fell short or went astray. There may still be much in it that reminds us of Cham's work, but it is as though his image upon it had been tarnished. That is how it now is with Creator's work. There is now a twist that should not be there, the results of something chosen.

"How I wish it were not so" the great man said, "the disease grows with a contagion so that you see the results of the drift you asked about all around—all the things that offend the Elohim One and ourselves." Nuach's eyes became heavy with moisture, and the lads thought they detected a weariness within them and within him. His tone and demeanor moved them also and they were silent, pondering.

"Let me express it another way" continues Nuach, gazing into a storied past in his mind, "we were once joined entirely to the Elohim. No gap existed. Then our first father and mother chose to join themselves to something else. Their act of independence immediately created a distance between us and him that cannot be crossed, at least, not by any of us, and it left a great deep alone-ness and hollowness within. But, as you know, when he seeks and finds a heart desiring to re-join him, he comes with what I can only call khane!"[2] He has told me that I have found khane in his sight!" The man's eyes suddenly seemed alight and bright with the khane of which he spoke and he smiled on his sons.

"Now I must tell you what I believe he has disclosed to me—and it is serious beyond anything we've ever known." The sons exchanged sidelong glances. Yefeth raised his eyebrows while Shem laid down the woven basket he had been repairing for his beloved wife. Something in Nuach's tone had signaled that a matter of great portent was about to be divulged. It was late afternoon now and so the four men washed hands and faces in cool water the women had brought recently from wells near their settlement. The sons knew that their father had telling things to share as they settled back in cushions and shared nuts and dates. The sun's heat had diminished as it slipped silently below western horizons and, as it went, beckoned to a cooling breeze which obediently came whispering and playing through their tents.

The son Shem, with a sense of building apprehension now spoke, "Father, what will happen? We have seen that no one listens to the story; no one wants to know that Elohim calls us to walk with him as benei ha Elohim—and that with him we can return to a measure of the first goodness. They laugh and deride and they make teraphim of their own to worship and say they are as good as

2. Khane is Hebrew for Grace

our Elohim One, but these just take them further away. With gods of their own invention they continue to eat and drink and debauch as though there will be no consequence."

The good father Nuach responded with, "well, if they laugh now, the derision will only intensify, because he has shown me what is going to happen."

"Meaning?" It was Shem again, but Cham also jumped in almost simultaneously with, "tell us more!"

"Violence[3] is what he has called it. He showed me and I saw that they have done violence to everything they learned from their fathers, like father Henoch whom Yahweh took away to himself without seeing death. Though they've been given fathers like this to follow, yet they've done violence to their own hearts, violence to truth, violence to right order—and violence to the voice within. They've corrupted their way and all day their hearts are intent only on the evil they can do.[4] They have even begun to call evil good and good, evil. That there can be such a strong delusion is a warning; and it has come by increment—the drift I spoke of—not all at once, just day upon day, time upon time as folk have succumbed to and followed the shadows of base inclinations and have done so with what they believe is impunity. Ah, but there are consequences, for inwardly their own hearts have become calloused to the voice and to the khane of Elohim and outwardly they are fracturing relationships and each other. It is a sad, sad time—and the more so because he has shown me that, as you have said, dear Shem, it is not without consequence. I believe with my inmost heart that he has said he must and will put an end to it; that the long and extended day of khane will be ended . . . but there is still time. It is late, but there is still time."

If the sons had looked quizzical and concerned before, they now stared at their father with a mix of incredulity and apprehension—"But father" broke in the young Yefeth, "we've been loyal to Creator! With your encouragement we've resisted the thing you

3. Genesis 6:11 where the Hebrew is KHAMAS, violence, malicious wrong-doing.

4. Genesis 6:5, 11, 12.

described so well as 'the drift'. We have seen his good hand on us and over us, as has all our family." The sons had wives and their alarm showed, until khane-filled Nuach shushed them.

He placed his deeply sun-browned hand on Shem's arm and spoke confidently and with the assurance borne of encounter with the One they called 'him' or 'he'.

"Here is what he has shown me. He will start again is the short version," he intoned, a new confidence rising as the truth that had been imprinted within now found form in words which he could hear coming from his lips with a surprising, calm authority, "Just as we are offended at what we see, his heart too, is broken. It's either finish it all or start again with new seed. One of the plans is to limit the days of life so that a boundary is placed on the runaway potential for darkness. Think of some of those we see nearby, like Machol, that man of treachery and deceit. He has seen more than two hundreds of summers and shows no sign of slowing. He leads many astray and is among the most debauched and influential of all—has a huge following. It was he who led the recent great surge in men and even women trying to procreate with the beasts. He has shown me that is why he will reduce our lives to five score and twenty years—and may reduce it again . . . . but that's not all . . . "

The boys leaned forward in anticipation, their faces a study in perplexity. They trusted their father and had seen the khane from Creator upon him and his ways. They were beneficiaries of Nuach's determination to be faithful. They too sensed the calm authority with which he was speaking. They knew it was truth; it bore witness within.

"He will bring a great and vast upheaval to the earth and a deluge from which we and ours will be given escape—but I am to warn the people. He has shown me his heart and oh, what a heart it is; not spoiled or inclined to darkness as ours can so easily be. No! His is a heart only and always of khane. He has blessed us and ours and kept us faithful so that the difference may be evident, but they, the benei adam, refuse to see . . . choose not to see. And for our rescue in the deluge to come I am to construct a great vessel which he has shown me in my heart. It will accommodate all creatures in pairs and food for them and the vessel will carry us and them across the great flooding waters and . . ."

The sons were incredulous. "But father, that would be huge beyond imagination" interrupted Shem, speaking for the three.

"Immense it is indeed," continued Nuach, "three hundreds of cubits in length, two score and ten wide and a score and ten high, to be exact. And you are familiar with the timber we use for our ploughs and implements? Some call it gopher. I am to use that because of its abundance and because it is light and easy to work—all for a vessel that we pray may not be necessary, if only the people will give heed." And so, Nuach went on to detail all that the Elohim One had shown him and his entranced sons sat in silent incredulity.

By and by it was Yefeth who raised his voice again, "but father, the animals are untamed and untouchable. How can you possibly believe that we'll be able to get them into this, this . . . this. . .imagined vessel, even if it is possible to build?" Skepticism was not usually a part of Yefeth's demeanor, especially to his father, but this stretched him and the brothers.

"Ah" says Nuach with a sigh; "I asked the same question and here's what came into my heart and mind and I knew it was from him. We have heard from our fathers the stories of the beginnings—of how it was before the Demise and the Banishment and how 'Dam and Chaveh communed with the animals and there was a sweet accord?" The boys nodded, somewhat un-persuaded. "Elohim intends to bring a special khane just as in those far back times—remember, the animals did not disobey, it was the man and the woman who chose independence. So, if the great vessel becomes necessary—if there is no change of heart among the benei adam, he will take care of all that. Besides, that will be a fitting start, will it not, to a new beginning for earth?"

The boys nodded again but said nothing, their minds churning with the incomprehensibility of what their father had unfolded to them . . . a vast deluge, a massive vessel, the animals coming and embarking! Yet they could tell that Nuach was utterly persuaded that it was *he* who had spoken and they knew their father well enough to know there would be no dissuading him. Nuach silently prayed for them to also hear the inner conviction voice so that they would fall in wholeheartedly with what was to be a vast project. He continued, "I am to build and warn, build and warn in the hope that the benei adam will turn back so that Elohim may spare them. He has given me a revelation of his heart and. . . .", he paused and almost shuddered as again the largeness and beauty of what he had experienced took hold within his deepest place, "his heart is so full, no. . . .over-flowing, with khane". Tears welled within his lustrous eyes again and blurred his vision and almost spilled and he wiped his eyes unashamedly with his loose linen sleeves as he continued to tell them of the plan and how it could be done and the pitch they could use for sealing between the squared timbers and how they would get the timbers to a site and the equipment they'd need to prepare and indeed where the building site would best be. And the boys began to get the vision and to say they would stand with their father while they continued to raise goats and till the land so that every need of the family was met while the great project proceeded. And soon the womenfolk came, anxious to know what occupied the four men so long, and called them to continue their talk over lentils and game and freshly baked bread, all washed down with water and with a rich rose-colored wine. It was an evening of mixed emotion and Nuach led the family in prayer aloud to the Great One to whom all their hearts seemed so warmly connected. And, they sensed right among them, The One who was Other!

And so, the days passed as they planned and began to build, and months then years passed and they stayed loyal and encouraged each other even as people derided and the project became a byword and an attraction for travelers and traders and all the settlements round about. And Nuach built and pleaded with the people who chose to grow the more strident in their mockery and their drunken debauchery and in their carelessness. There were even those who attempted to thwart the building or to burn the great vessel and to spoil the work, but there was a protection over the work and over Nuach's family. And then the day came, as eventually come all things spoken by the great Yahweh and anticipated, and the mockers watched in awe and wondered how the man had such control over beasts and animals as they came as of their own accord and entered the huge vessel through the opening in its side. It was a wonder and yet they continued in their lustful ways. And the debauched people were witnessing firsthand the working of the khane they were rejecting. Mockery and resistance and unbelief, not to mention addiction to their ways, had calloused their eyes to its reality. Surely all things would continue as they ever had. The Sun would rise tomorrow and the grass would grow and, more importantly, the wine would flow. Any qualms brought about by the presence of the great construction and the pleading of its constructors could soon be quenched with more wine and beer and licentious indulgence. Blindness begat blindness; depravity begat greater depravity until, as the One known much later in your human time as Son of Man put it, "the deluge came, and carried them all away."[5]

The khane that wise Nuach had himself found had been spurned by the benei adam and so an end came and a separation came. The old had passed away; behold all things became new, after darkness came light. And with the light, a new people, a restoration people bringing humankind back . . . yes, back from the brink and once more in the direction of the unspoiled state in which it was . . . at the Beginning. The stream of the benei ha Elohim would continue to flow.

I, Watcher Shaqaad have seen all this unfold in the realm you call time and I worship the Mighty One Yahweh Elohim together with these benei ha Elohim with whom I have developed a strange sense of oneness though we are of such different worlds. I see, but do not comprehend, how Yahweh Elohim is dealing with this extraordinary class of beings—and especially those whose hearts are inclined to him. It is a wonder!

And now, to one of the most outstanding examples of these Sons of Elohim. Outstanding because Yahweh chose him to exemplify the thing both he and you call faith. I will have him speak for himself . . .

---

5. Jesus in Matthew 24:39. The Greek word translated flood is kataklusmos (see also 2 Peter 3:5,6).

Part Two: **Which People?**

CHAPTER 5

Apart-ness in embryo:
the incarnation idea

"I AM IVRAHIM. MY birth name was Avram, and, as many who
read these words will know, my name was changed. Not by me. No:
it was he, who said, just as clearly as I hear words from those I love,
'your name will no more be called Avram, but your name shall be
Ivrahim; for I have made you a father of many nations!' To say that
I was astonished is understatement indeed for I had already fallen
face-down in his presence! And then to hear him transmit these
words into my deepest place so that it became impossible for me
to doubt them, was extraordinary. I say transmit, because at one
moment no words were there and in the next instant they were
unmistakably within and what's more, in-erasable. Mind you, it
was not the first time this had occurred, but it is always indubi-
table. And at once I saw what the new name meant. My old name,
which meant in the tongue of you who read, High Father, I had
more than once felt to be beyond my worth or ability to attain; but
this new name! Why, it blew me away completely, for it at once
educed and captured all that he had been saying to me from ages
ago—from the time when I left Charran and he said he'd make a
people of me, if you please! I can scarcely describe both the hum-
bling and the lifting up I sensed together, as it transfused into my
spirit. And with a 'knowing' that it would be, even as he had said.
In fact, he spoke as I'd never heard anyone speak before; as though
the thing of which he spoke, was already accomplished! For when
he told me my new name, he said it this way, "I *have made you* a

father of many nations."[1] He spoke of what was already accomplished before it started! This is mystery indeed to me, and yet my heart responds with a deep 'ahmeen' because I know I am strangely connected into purposes bigger and greater than time, and that he can indeed speak of promised things as already accomplished! And the new name? It was to be henceforth, Ivrahim—Father of a multitude of nations!

"But I am old now and have walked my walk; yet I remember as yesterday the time when he called me to leave my land and my kindred and my father's household. It was a big ask and yet accompanied by such an enabling word of promise that it hardly seemed like a decision. To be blessed and made into a great nation and to become a blessing to all the nations on earth! It was then that I began to get an inkling of his idea of difference. My dear father Terach, blessed be his name, had set out from Ur of the Kasdimah[2] to go to Kna'an but he settled in Charran[3] and worshipped other gods.[4]

"I am saddened that he did not complete what he set out to do, but it was from that same place, yes, Charran, that my Yahweh called me and I had to separate myself from Father Terach and my own people and complete the journey so that his plan to demonstrate difference could advance. I know that those who follow will see an ongoing fulfilment of his promise to me and I am blessed that my son Yitzchaq, the one promised long ago by Yahweh Elohim, has found such a good woman and wife in Ribhqeh—and one of such rare beauty! What a story of his providence that is, as I sent my trusted servant to find a woman from the people of my original country rather than from among the people of Kna'an. Though I know my Shadday[5] has brought us here I did not want Yitzchaq to be compelled to marry among those who worship

1. Genesis 17:5

2. Chaldeans

3. Charran (Haran) means Main Road or Road Junction—perhaps a comfortable place to settle.

4. See Joshua 24:2

5. Almighty

strange gods. It has become clearer and clearer to me as life passes that there is but one Elohim; and it has become evident to me how far so many of his creatures have departed from him again, into ways and means of their own. They know not what they do as they invent gods and then bow to their inventions! I have observed and learned that these manufactured gods do indeed have power to deceive and corrupt, and lead many on a downward spiral into confusion. Their idol inventions indeed become inhabited only too obligingly by dark and deceptive powers. I have seen that there are other voices behind the images and they are not the voice of Yahweh. They are voices that allure with offers of that which they can never fulfil, for they have not that power, only the power of deceptive promise. Our great Yahweh is the only one who can both speak with his mouth and fulfil with his hand! Praised be his everlasting name!

"The longer I live, the more I desire to obey only the voice that leads to shalom and multiplication. I see the widening gap between those who hear and follow his voice and those who follow the other voices. I see too, that there must be a gap, for we cannot go their way. No! Once having heard his voice, and having followed, we cannot cross to that other side without grave damage; we cannot return from being the benei ha Elohim. That choice would be self-destructive, for shalom is here. Certainty is here; here is purpose and here is fulfilment, as what he says comes to pass and fills our lives. And nor can they who heed other voices cross to this side—at least not without relinquishing their manufactured gods and vain imaginings. Most assuredly he would receive them also as benei ha Elohim then. I have seen that it is so, blessed be his name! Oh—and I see that it is his 'otherness'—the chasm of difference between us and him that he wants to close so that we too, become joined to *his*. It's only in this that we are distinguished ever more clearly as his sons and people—The People—who know him and with whom he dwells! The People who've chosen to walk where he walks and to turn their back on the self-destructive ways of the Goyim. They too, are a demonstration; they, of the downward slide to depravity and bankruptcy of character that accompanies the choice to listen to other voices.

"Indeed, what a Yahweh he is! I have seen that he covers our nakedness, fills our hollowness and swallows up our inadequacy! I still hear those words he spoke in the hills of Moriah so long ago, 'Yahweh Yireh', LORD who foresees, LORD of *pro*-vision![6] And I have found him to be the One who is always seeing ahead, preparing for me in all times and places. I've come to understand that it is in his heart to renew as fully as possible what our father 'Dam and mother Chaveh lost. So, I too, and those with me choose to join with his *otherness*. It is a privilege. I see that in choosing, day by day, we become joined to his purpose to display difference! I see it! I see it! Yes, he must have a people who are *other*—making difference visible; and indeed, desirable. Let it be Yahweh Elohim! And let it be through my children and their children after them, that amidst the darkness of the benei adam, the light of Yahweh Yireh, the One I know also as Shadday, is desired—across the gap!"

6. Genesis 22:8–14

CHAPTER 6

Apart-ness visible

I KNEW YOU WOULD enjoy hearing first hand from the great Ivrahim. Because he believed, Yahweh has called him his beloved friend![1] My watching has caused me to understand that it is a merciful kindness that Yahweh has implemented this plan. Though I know not this thing that Yahweh calls sin, yet I have observed its product. There is a thing that occurs whenever one of the benei ha Elohim moves in a direction other than that of Yahweh. It is similar to the change I saw at the beginning, when 'Dam and Chaveh desired independence. A shadow falls where light has been and the pathway becomes indistinct and confused, crowded alternately with thorns and swamps. And I have seen the sadness and longing that at once comes upon Yahweh's heart. Then too—I've pondered the thing called faith that brings you and him together when choice is made to turn from the shadow. This is mysterious to me, it appears that when at first you have inclination to choose light, this 'faith' seems to arrive as a gift arrives; and yet the gift, in turn, appears to also be enabling the choice! I have seen also, that when he speaks to one of you distinctly, his words are enabling words; they carry within them this thing called faith. Of these mysteries, I find I cannot speak, as I say, for they are outside the gamut of our ministry and realm. We do only as Yahweh directs and on occasions those directions impel us into your time realm and affairs as you will see. But to return to my point, kindness, yes, and not to you only, but to all peoples. For it pleases him to have among

---

1. 2 Chronicles 20:7, Isaiah 41:8 & James 2:23

the goyim, a people who make truth visible—the undeniability of his being and working; that is, for any and for all who have eyes to see and ears to hear and a desire to know! For those, this thing called faith arrives. It is . . . how shall I put it? . . . a 'fleshing' of his real-ness—yes, that is his desire; a tangible way for all in the earth to see that he's real and that he is there.

But I see that one featured in your annals desires to speak more of these things. Better that one from your realm gives voice . . .

"Oh—allow me to introduce myself! I am Yitzchak; yes, that Yitzchak, son of Ivrahim the Great, and I have seen it, first in my father Ivrahim and now, in my own journey (though often weak and forgetful) as I endeavor to hear and follow as one of the benei ha Elohim. Oh yes, how I have seen it. Why, from that never-to-be-forgotten day for the ages with my father at The Place[2] and in all our lives after that, I have seen, dimly at first and now more clearly, the Plan! Let me tell you of a recent incident in which, I must say, I had begun to wonder what his purpose could be.

"For you see, we had a famine in our land and there was nothing for it but to seek help elsewhere or watch as my family and flocks perished. This, despite all that he had said to me about provision and about the two nations in my beautiful wife Ribhqeh's womb. In the severity of the situation I was of a mind to travel to Mistrayim[3] where there was plenty, but, in the brightness of his kindness Yahweh appeared to me, if you please, and told me not to go down to Mitsrayim! He seems to make sure that we hear from him if our heart is truly to follow him! It was a mercy and a very great surprise and blessing. He indicated that I should stay in the region of Gerar among the Pliŝtim[4] people whose king was one, Avimélekh. There, I have to say, I did exactly as my father had done about his wife and our mother, Sarai. Yes, I too was untruthful to Avimélekh about Ribhqeh my wife. For fear of being killed for her

2. The Place—ha makom in Hebrew was the sacred site visited by Abraham, Isaac, Jacob and others which became known as Bethel, House of God and where the temples were later erected. See this author's book, THE PLACE.

3. Egypt, Genesis 26:2

4. Philistine

by the men of that place, I told Avimélekh she was my sister[5] and in this I did not behave as a true bene ha Elohim. Yes, this was somewhat self-serving and left her vulnerable; may Yahweh have mercy on my weakness! In any case it was a folly because Avimélekh looked from his window one day and saw me caressing my darling Ribhqeh and my deceit was uncovered.[6] Yet, despite even this, Yahweh has been true to his covenant with my father and me and has blessed us in this place. Blessed us to the extent that Avimélekh and the Plištim people have *seen it* with their eyes and even *said it* with their lips![7] Our presence and the obvious hand of our Yahweh on us has had its usual divisive effect, for while some have marveled, others have begun to make trouble by blocking the wells dug by my father Ivrahim.

"I see that it seems to be his way—that is, to make it obvious that he's around and available—always providing opportunity for choice. I am sensing that this is how it will always be: he makes it clear by demonstration, and for those who'll take heed he will make a way for them to become benei ha Elohim; and those who reject the obvious he will allow to continue trying to make their own way as benei adam. It is a grace and I am not troubled by it for I am seeing as I look back and try to look forward that we have been chosen as the demonstration of his nature and character. How else will it be seen unless it is through Ha Am (The People)— the benei ha Elohim who follow and who have chosen—and yet mysteriously have also been chosen, for his purpose?"

---

5. Genesis 26:7

6. Genesis 26:8–9

7. Genesis 26:28 "We have certainly seen that the LORD is with you"

Part Three: **The Journey**

CHAPTER 7

The Forge and its Product

> But the LORD has taken you and brought you out of the
> iron furnace, out of Egypt, to be **His people**, an inheri-
> tance, as you are this day (Deuteronomy 4:20 NKJV; see
> also Jeremiah 11:4 NKJV **emphasis** added)

IT IS WHAT YOU would call in your time realm, a long story, the one
about how you came to be in such a predicament in Mitsrayim (or
Egypt as you know it in your day and language) and under the hand
of a P'aroh who knew not your champion, Yoseff. A long yet event-
ful story; one foretold to your Father Ivrahim! Yes, foretold by the
One who made himself known to Ivrahim as Foreseeing Yahweh.
For I have observed that those who keep the stories have recorded
that long ago, Yahweh spoke to him when he was still known as
Avram. For, at the incident of the covenant-cutting when Yahweh
spoke and Avram believed, this is what was said; 'know for certain
that your descendants will be strangers in a country not their own
and will be enslaved and mistreated and after 400 years . . .they
will come out with great possessions and they'll come back here
. . .when the sin of the Amorites has reached full measure.'[1] It was a
hard message, but it was there in Mitsrayim that your people-hood
was forged, for you went there first in Yoseff, as but one, in the
remarkable providence of Yahweh—yes, *that* Yoseff who had been
sold by his brothers and yet became First Minister to the great
P'aroh of Mitsrayim. It is a story of Yahweh being just the same for
Yoseff as he was for Father Ivrahim; Yahweh Yireh. It is a story of a
family comprising but seventy persons, growing into a people in a

1. Genesis 15:9–16

41

land strange to them! Indeed, you were given land for your flocks and herds in G'shen and it was not until your great Yoseff and what he had done for Mitsrayim was forgotten that things became bitter for you.

I see that all this was his way of forging you into The People who would exit that land with great wealth and power demonstrating his sovereignty over *all* nations! But there was an event (and I was one of those commissioned by the Elohim One to be involved closely in it)—a singular event by which Yahweh separated you as his people, The People, to continue the witness as the benei ha Elohim.

Pesakh—Separation event!

What a day! Oh, what a day! It was something even for me, one of the Watchers to behold; one who has seen things not, as yet, permitted to you humans. It became etched forever in everyone's minds and in the collective consciousness of The People, but here is Shelemiya, one of Moshe's seventy whose assignment it was to record the events. He will explain the great event that separated you from Mitsrayim!

"Yes, I am Shelemiya, one of the seventy chosen to assist lord Moshe in the government of this great people whom Yahweh has so dramatically made his own. It is not easy to describe the place that the passing over on the night of our deliverance holds in every heart and mind. Indeed, it was the single event that separated us from those who possessed and oppressed us in servitude; for it was we, yes, we who applied the lamb's blood to our houses—at the doorway which separates inside from outside—who were delivered! Outside, the angel of death, the one called Abaddon-Destroyer swept through G'shen and Mitsrayim to take the firstborn of those who had not prepared with the blood of an unblemished lamb. Inside the houses signified by that blood, all lived! He is indeed at one and the same time both an Elohim of mercy and an Elohim of justice! It is a mystery. But I see that this was the event, at the end of the forging, which brought forth new iron in the form of a new people—The People—separated to Yahweh forever just as he had told Father Ivrahim![2] At that event—that moment in time, we became separated from Mitsrayim, to be henceforth I believe, a different and contrasting people. I am to record the events for Moshe because we have been instructed by Yahweh to keep an annual feast as a memorial of this extraordinary moment—ha Pesakh (or the Passover in the reader's language). Praised be the everlasting Yahweh!

2. Genesis 15:13–14

CHAPTER 8

Men in white garments

... you shall be a special treasure to Me above all people
*... and you shall be to Me a kingdom of priests and **a holy***
nation(Exodus 19:5 & 6 NKJV ***emphasis*** added)

HERE IS A BEAUTIFUL encounter I witnessed that I, Shaqaad, want
to share with you: it is a strange thing for me, from a different
realm, to find myself describing things within your realm. And
yet it brings a sense of awe as I behold the wonder of a creature
who (I am privileged to see so clearly), is made in the semblance
and likeness of Elohim. Analogous! I see that he describes himself
to you in your terms—as though he were one of you, having eyes
and ears and hands and feet. And I know that he does see and hear
and perform and go, even as you are enabled to in your realm. The
thing that you have which I and the hosts like me do not, is this
image-within correspondence. It is an 'I am' that he has put within
each of you that is just like his! I see too, that yours is a realm that
is temporary, even though time is not meaningful to me; I think I
understand that some things are destined by him to have what you
call a beginning and an end—and can be sustained in a state of
existence only as he desires and permits. We see that he is holding
it all together and in that state for his own purpose, which will,
believe me, be fulfilled. But allow me to try to bring you a description of this particular encounter because I think it will help you
understand what is happening:

The bright, mid-afternoon sun, glared off stark linen which
had been whitened by expert craftsmen. The procession in white
made its way into the outer court of a fabric enclosure standing in

the middle of a vast encampment. The encampment itself stood in a near-perfect array around the fabric enclosure. The strange enclosure itself was some fifty of your meters in length and perhaps twenty-five meters wide and within it stood, towards its western end, another tent which appeared to be made of animal skins.

The twelve-year-old lad spoke to his uncle with an incredulous tone for, although he had witnessed the scene before, it had, up till now, been part of the routine of life in the camp and largely taken for granted by his childish mind. But this day was different. For some reason, new interest was generated. Perhaps it was due to the perspective afforded from the low hillside above and to the north of the camp where he sat with his uncle. The lad, Hillel, had been exploring the landscape with favorite Uncle Nachum, a good man who had taken a special interest in the lad, whose father had died a year back when bitten by a serpent during the great discouragement near Edom.[1]

"Why do the priests dress like that, my Uncle—and all that stuff they do, what does it all mean?" To which Nachum's first thought was, where do I begin?

"You need some history, Hillel . . . you need a little history!" Nachum said as he stripped the leaves and blue flowers from a handful of hyssop he had plucked as they wandered. As he massaged the leaves and flowers in his hands the pungent camphor-like aroma claimed their nostrils and added to the bright afternoon euphoria. He retained a small bunch to take home for his wife to use, for it made a nice addition to broths as well as making their humble tent smell of outdoors.

Learning

"So", he continued, "I'll begin with our great leader Moshe. When Yahweh called him to lead our liberation from Mitsrayim, he also gave him Ahron—and you'll see why in a moment, for Yahweh told lord Moshe that we had been chosen for a great task that

1. Numbers 21:7–9

would be significant for all the peoples of the earth! From the very early days, before father Ivrahim, we who choose the path of Yahweh have been known as benei ha Elohim. Those who choose independence from him are known as benei adam."

"You mean all of us here, out in the wilds with no country or city or real homes like others have, are benei ha Elohim?" The lad was as incredulous as he was bright. He was just old enough to remember fragments of life in Mitsrayim—and their home there, albeit under a hard taskmaster in the P'aroh, and of their flight into the wastelands. He remembered the massive edifices of Mitsrayim and the cruelty . . . "then if we are so special, if we are benei ha Elohim, what are we doing here—with nothing but this tabernacle thing and all our tents and moving all the time . . . ?" His voice had somehow overtaken his thoughts before he realized he was articulating them aloud. Uncle Nachum detected a precocious tone in the lad, but let it pass lest he respond inappropriately. He knew this was going to be hard to explain! Hillel sat restlessly and picked up nearby pebbles to throw at prominent rocks that bumped out of the hillside below them, looking to his fertile imagination like grotesque and wild animals. The pebbles pinged off the hard surfaces and rolled down the slope disturbing an occasional skink that skittered away to find safety beneath a stone or the dried bones of a long-dead goat. Everything, including the afternoon sun seemed to await Nachum's reply, as the boy added, almost insolently—

"So, when do we get to be special?" He couldn't see what was so special about drifting around untamed wastelands—and had already seen enough reasonably comfortable settlements in more amenable territory to create questions in his agile mind. But the uncle decided to let the boy's words fall to the ground for the moment and simply smiled in gracious acknowledgement; the sun and the child could both wait. They continued to pick their way silently down the slope, avoiding loose stones that could so easily roll under sandaled feet and cause a fall and before long, the sudden, sharp sound of the blast of a shofar caught their attention. The primal sound shook out over the local geography, calling, it seemed, more than humankind, to acknowledge Yahweh. It seemed too, to be calling the very elements. It was time for the evening sacrifice. That was why the procession of priests was making its solemn way into the courtyard of the enclosure. As Nachum watched the procedure he had seen so often, it prompted a response to his nephew's youthful ignorance. It formed as a question:

"Hillel—it was you who used the word 'special'. Why?"

The lad answered that his father had taught him that with Pesakh and then Yam Suph,[2] Yahweh had separated the children of Ysra-El, (once known as Yaakov), to be a people—The People, of his own . . . whatever that meant! "Father told me that the separation really happened at Pesakh with the blood on our door-posts and lintels; but if we've just been separated to live as nomads how can that help anyone?"

"Ah", says Nachum, trying to explain as carefully as he could the reason for their wandering; "you see, Yahweh took us quite quickly to the southern borders of a beautiful land that was to be ours but most of the spies sent in to assess it came back fearful and they made the people fearful and faithless. There were only two, Yeshua and K'leb who believed that the extraordinary event at Yam Suph should encourage us to know he was with us in a way that meant we could easily overcome the evil ones who occupied that territory. I'm afraid that even my own heart was swayed by the cry of the majority, who wanted, would you believe, to go back to Mitsrayim! It was because we did not trust the great Yahweh, even after he showed himself so mighty, that we are now in this awful predicament. I am ashamed my dear nephew, of my own heart in this, and I have learned from it how easily we can be swayed from strong confidence, into doubt and fear." They sat silently as the young boy digested what his uncle had said. Nachum felt like apologizing to the boy because he could see that it was his own unbelief along with that of others that had consigned his generation to its fruit. Hillel felt almost uncomfortable because he admired his uncle greatly. He was learning that everyone—even those we admire most, have weaknesses and doubts just like his own. Nachum placed his assuring hand on the lad's shoulder and

2. The Red Sea

said, "the important thing, Hillel, is that we learn about Yahweh's dealings with us. He is the Teacher and we must all become better learners and choose to whom we listen." A long pause followed as some tears of regret welled up in Uncle Nachum's eyes and he looked away to the west and north; to the direction of promise. Slowly and courageously he resumed with, "now it is to you and your generation to be strong, courageous and full of belief that our Yahweh is able to do everything he has said—and more! He who brought us out of Mitsrayim and through Yam Suph with such an incredible deliverance and then brought water and food all these years is well able to take you in to what he has promised. Hillel, it is the promise that is all important. You must know that when he speaks, he will fulfil . . . even when there's a delay." He then added thrice more, with at first a somewhat wistful voice and then with changing emphasis and strengthening certainty, "*he* will fulfil . . . he *will* fulfil . . . he will *fulfil!*"

Now young Hillel's heart beat with a new admiration for his humble, honest uncle who returned to his thread about Yeshua and K'leb . . . .

"Indeed, I know these men and soon I will introduce you to them—for being with them will, I know, encourage your heart."

Hillel was prompted to ask Uncle Nachum more about these two because he had heard bits and pieces about them around the camp. And his uncle shared with him the promise given to K'leb about being one who would see and inherit in Kn'aan . . . one day. Nachum then wisely moved forward with this;

"And why do you suppose the priests and their assistants the Levites dress in such pure white garments?"[3]

---

3. Exodus 28:40–42 'The ordinary priests wear four garments all year round-these are the same as the "white garments" worn by the High Priest on the Day of Atonement: tunic, pants, hat, and belt. Referring to these priests, the verse states "And for Aaron's sons you shall make for them tunics, and you shall make for them belts, and you shall make for them hats. . . and make for them linen pants. . . "(Ex. 28:40–42). These garments are to be made from flax, and they too must be created from threads consisting of six individual strands' (from The Temple Institute site https://www.templeinstitute.org/priestly_garments.htm

"I was told that it is because that is what Yahweh is like and the priests stand for Him."

"That is so—and it is more than that, for it is also what we are to be like as The People who represent him to the Goyim. The priests represent him to us . . . and us to him. Indeed, they are a picture. How will others know about the cleanness and purity of Yahweh unless there is a reminder in visual form and it is also displayed through us? Moshe has said that Yahweh told him we are to be a whole kingdom of priests and a separated people.[4]

"And of course, we also need that constant reminder that the One we are dealing with is . . . how shall I express it? . . . Other! Yes, that's it. He is the separate One, the One who is completely 'other'; dwelling in a separate, un-tarnished state—and yet, here among us. Untouchable! Yet close, with us! That is why he has put his presence in the most holy place, right there in the tent below us. It is marvelous—he dwells there between the kheruvim at the mercy seat above the chest containing his Law–Word." Nachum used the Hebrew word qodesh (in the reader's tongue, holy or consecrated other) with a noticeably hushed tone. He was a man who knew what the presence of the holy meant.

He continued in the same reverential tone that was also edged with a sense of wonder and indeed, excitement, "Hillel, the older I get, the more I marvel at the meaning of the tent in the middle of our camp—for he is there, *with* his people; not far away in heaven, but on the journey with us as the Guide, Protector, Provider, as . . . ," But he was interrupted by the inquisitive Hillel—

"Well where is the land he's taking us to; and what's it like? And tell me again what happens in the Tent and with the High Priest and with the sacrifice and the laver and . . . ." Now it was the uncle's turn to interrupt!

4. Exodus 19:5–6

Heart call

"Not so fast, not so fast young man; there is much to tell and it can-not all be told at once. The telling is also a journey." He gathered his thoughts; how to take this lad he loved so much on the journey that led into the embrace of Yahweh—and indeed to embracing Yahweh with his whole being—as one of the benei ha Elohim?

I, Watcher Shaqaad was enthralled at what the boy's uncle saw and said next. It was like this:

Overhead, a flock of wild barburim (known to you who read, as geese) flew southward across spare and almost grassless hills. The sight gave Nachum inspiration—

"You see those beautiful barburim flying to where it is warmer and where there is food?" He indicated aloft with his bearded chin and Hillel's gaze lifted immediately from the scene below to the brightness of the azure sky southward. He lifted his sun-browned left hand to shade his squinting eyes as they locked onto the mar-velous sight. Against the uninterrupted blue of the sky, the pristine white of the plumage was stark and impossible to miss, especially as the great birds had not yet gained significant altitude.

Nachum continued, "How do they know where to go? What calls them to the place they should be?" The question was designed to make the boy think before answering.

"It's just something they know inside?" said Hillel a little querulously, "something that calls them?"

"Aha", says uncle Nachum, "now you're onto something. Yes . . . it seems Creator has implanted something within them that is a knowing, without any contemplation or consideration—and which they do not resist."

"You mean like it calls them to do it—and to go there . . . and they just go?"

"Yes! And just as they are drawn to that which is good and best for them, Yahweh has put something within us too that calls and draws . . . to *him*; calls us to the whiteness and separateness found only in him, for that's where he wants us to be—and it is actually where our hearts deeply desire to be. It's a place of shalom and protection." The twelve-year-old began to pay attention as he tore his gaze away from the vanishing barburim to look intently into his uncle's dark eyes that shone with a luster like amethyst from the shadowed slots between thick eyebrows above and thicker beard below. Although he had seen fifty or more summers his hair had not yet greyed and it shone black in the afternoon sunshine. Nachum continued to tell the boy about the priests and their rosters and duties and all the requirements for their life. He told him of the meaning of the laver and the ceremonial washing and the sacrifices and the altar of incense and the clothing of the priests, all the while emphasizing *qodesh* and its meaning for daily life, Hillel nodding and occasionally posing bright questions as understanding began to take hold, not just in his mind but throughout his entire being. He began to feel drawn, like the barburim his uncle had used as a metaphor, to the apart-ness that beckoned; to being, like Yahweh, different and other—for the sake both of Yahweh and of the nations that Yahweh desired also to draw. The boy listened intently as Nachum told him of Yom Kippur (the Day of Atonement) and what it meant to the people—and he made sure Hillel understood about the seriousness of sin. He made sure he grasped the idea that the priests stood between Yahweh and the people— representing both to each other; on the one hand representing Yahweh to the people, and on the other, representing the people to Yahweh! He said, "This is why they are so important and why they must be qodesh for our great Yahweh has said of us all, 'you shall be qodesh for I am qodesh'. The apart-ness is of very great importance because The People are the illustration of the life of Yahweh! We are the qodesh people; we are, in a sense, the face of Yahweh to the nations! He has intentionally separated us to himself." Nachum found himself excited and preaching to the rapt Hillel! He found the telling of truth exhilarating and faith-building.

"So" says the enthralled Hillel, "what happens when we break a commandment or disobey Yahweh?"

"Ah" says the uncle, "In his great mercy he has made a way to deal with our sin so that we should not suffer its awful consequence. For he has said that it brings death—and by that he means separation of a different kind; separation from his presence and blessings." With wisely crafted words Nachum walked the pre-teenager through the sacrifices that Yahweh had ordained for The People, his Ysra-El. As the aromas from the enclosure below wafted up on a soft and fickle breeze, he told him of the great sacrifice on Yom Kippur and of the daily sacrifices, keeping it as uncomplicated as he could and ensuring that the lad understood why sacrifice was necessary—and the meaning behind each one.

Then Nachum told all about the great Feasts, of which of course young Hillel was very aware but knew not the full significance of each and how they were for remembrance of Yahweh's interventions and his blessings in the life of The People. He explained again to the now rapt boy, who toyed with the locks of his tightly curled and dark brown hair, how Pesakh had begun. Nachum himself was some seven years younger when The People came out of Mitsrayim, but he made the story live for Hillel who hardly shifted his gaze from the face or the hand gestures of his now highly animated uncle—Hillel could almost see the waters closing over the chariots of Mitsrayim! Nachum went on to unpack the reason for the Chag HaMotzi (Feast of Unleavened Bread) and then Reshit Katzir (First-fruits) and Shavu'ot (Pentecost) with the arrival of Torah and . . . .

"Did you see the mountain ablaze?" interrupted the lad.

"Oh yes, oh yes" says Nachum, lowering his voice at the memory of the awe of the moment, "but we could only stand near the foot of the mountain for Moshe had set a boundary which we were not to pass, on pain of death. But there was such a noise and a quaking and visible fire that we feared for the life of our great leader. It was a day no-one could ever forget! Believe me when Yahweh comes near and speaks in such a way you don't miss it, nor do you forget!"

"And what of Ahron and the calf of gold?" queried Hillel, at which his uncle winced and replied with regret and a sense of shame in his voice for he did not want to speak of it— "It was a folly . . . to think that even Ahron along with so many could sink so quickly, having seen that Yahweh was at work up there in the mountain with our Moshe; having heard the voice and seen the fire and trembled with fear, why did we fall? Oh, it was a hasty and tragic folly!" As though to emphasize Nachum's shame, a dark and heavy cloud suddenly rolled in from the west, bringing a pall of deep shadow across the previously dazzling landscape—and a surprisingly fierce chill. The lad felt it and shuddered, for the significance of the moment was not lost to him. And then he returned to his questioning—

"But what did Yahweh say to Moshe about us, the children of Yaakov? I heard that he told him we are special."

"It is so"—and the wise uncle watched the heavy cloud roll eastward to give permission again for the westering Sun to take up where it had been before being interrupted, bringing again its unabashed light onto the priestly whiteness below. The whiteness contrasted with the greens and browns of the hills and earth around the priests. Nachum and Hillel had paused again and sat on a large, flat rock not far from the bottom of the hill as Nachum gathered again his thoughts before responding with—

"Moshe has told us—and there are those who have been commissioned to record it—that our great Yahweh told something like this, 'You've all seen what I did to Mitsrayim, and how I carried you on eagles' wings to bring you to myself. If you obey me fully and keep my covenant, then among all nations, you are going to be my treasured own and deeply valued property. Even though the whole earth is mine, you're going to be my very own kingdom of priests and a qodesh nation.'[5]

"And Moshe was told to speak all these words to us, and indeed he did and we had to prepare ourselves with washing of souls and of garments for two days before his visitation. And that's when he came—and gave his standards for living, the laws which, when lived by would distinguish us as his! But yes, imagine Hillel, a nation unlike any other and chosen to be different and special so that all nations could come and see. It is a terrifying call and obligation; you must take it seriously, dear nephew."

5. Exodus 19:4–6

And with that the uncle and nephew, as though by agreed signal, rose and began the walk back to the camp, all the while keeping an eye on the activity in the enclosure and playfully pushing each other off the wild goat track that meandered aimlessly through rocky outcroppings to a very small, almost waterless streamlet below.

CHAPTER 9

Being Moshe—and the nuach promise

*By faith Moses, when he became of age, refused to be called the son of Pharaoh's daughter, choosing rather to suffer affliction with **the people** (Ha Am) of God than to enjoy the passing pleasures of sin, esteeming the reproach of Christ greater riches than the treasures in Egypt; for he looked to the reward* (Hebrews 11:24–26 NKJV **emphasis** and parenthesis added)

IT WAS MORNING AND Moshe was seated on a prominence overlooking the camp, with that most beautiful tent there in its center wherein resided the ark and the tablets and the kheruvim with the very Presence *he* had promised would go with them.

The day and the light and the autumn sun gave shimmering life and vibrancy to the acacias and palms surrounding the wadi near which they had camped. Insects flew and scurried and buzzed about the business that ever occupies insects. The light played on tiny bodies and translucent wings and activity. What was it about light at this season of your earth that made things appear different than under harsher summer sun? The angle and the play of autumn light seemed to educe a certain mood in natural things that spoke thankfulness, but also expectation. To humans it was like a sigh of contentment at the pleasantness of that in-between state of dismissed summer harshness and on-coming winter chill. It found in Moshe a sense of reverie and a mingling of expectation and, strangely—disappointment. Disappointment at some of the stubbornness of his people, indeed The People—but also expectation of Yahweh's leading. The cloud would move again. It was, indeed, an adventure to trust him! Moshe's musing to himself continued . . . .

I cannot say why he has so singularly blessed me: I, a man who has killed and had things in my heart that have not brought him pleasure. But this only tells me more about his heart than about mine; and, I am forever learning about his heart and that it is not like mine and, oh how pleased I am that it is so! He has used a word, as I have communed with Him . . . it is a word I have come to delight in, indeed, feel secure in. It is, in our language, khesed, with that back-of-the-throat sound my people love to hear, on the 'kh'. I believe it is hard to take its meaning into another language. It is rendered in many ways, such as loyalty and loving-kindness and covenant love or faithfulness. . . . and all of them are correct! It describes his relent-less determination to help and to bless which, (I've discovered) he ever exhibits toward me and The People . . . and indeed to any who will join him. I remember clearly those early days of my discovery of him and my choosing to flow with his choosing of me! How at the bush that burned so strangely as did also, I have to say, my heart within me! And then the unmistakable commission and my abject sense of inadequacy. Me? To stand before the P'aroh and make de-mands? But first I had to stand before the elders of my own people. I sometimes think that was the more difficult task. But you had told me what to say; 'tell them I AM has sent me.' Yet somehow when you said that Name it found an answer from my deepest heart . . . from my own I am . . . and there settled upon me a knowing as I'd not ever known anything before! There was the deepest 'ah-meen' arising from my very own 'I am' and I knew you would carry the day. And . . . you did it; you did it! And I was borne along in it all by power and certitude that was not my own. You gave everything I needed for the task you had asked of me—hallelu-Yah and blessed be your name, oh Yahweh!

And as we journeyed together in this grand adventure of your-choosing-combined-with-my-choice, I came to see with the greatest clarity that you were separating to yourself a people, a 'qodesh' people just as you had promised the fathers. As I made choice to be one with your choice, so The People you were separating were asked to do the same! And Ahron and I and the elders were being carried on your great tide that no power on earth could stop—indeed, on eagle's wings as you said. They tried, Yahweh, oh how they tried; how P'aroh expended all within his power to prevent the work of your hand, yet how futile it was. For you had decreed it, and you always fulfil with your hand that which you speak with your mouth—blessed be your all-powerful name! I learned long ago that what you intend will be, and your intention is a people known by your name, The People of Elohim and Yahweh. The People for whom Elohim contends—Ysra-El;[1] The People who would not need to contend for themselves but for whom you did the fighting; The People distinctive because of this.

"Moshe my lord!" The interruption to his prayerful reverie gave him a start even though the voice was so familiar! He rose to greet Yeshua, that faithful, chosen servant, who has all these years supported and defended Moshe. He continued, "sometimes I wonder why the great Yahweh has chosen us."

The interruption was fortuitous for it enabled Moshe to bring Yeshua in, exactly where his ponderings had taken him and so he gave them voice as they walked together down the slope toward the wadi and its shade because the sun was now hot.

Yeshua continued, "And yet, as faltering as we so often seem to be, his disposition toward us always plays out in kind provision and action toward us—for they are all khesed and nothing but khesed, yes . . . that expresses it best". As they arrived beneath the shade of the palms and acacias Moshe led Yeshua to a spot that had become a favorite over the last few weeks. Yahweh had held their camp in this location for some months now and Moshe had begun to enjoy it so much that he knew he would almost be disappointed when next the cloud moved and it was time to depart. As they approached, they startled some grey doves drinking at one of the pools in the wadi and their swift wings thrummed and whirred, carrying them upward to hide amidst the green fronds. Yeshua motioned to a dappled patch where sun and shade wrestled

1. Ysra-El means God contends

for dominion as the fronds overhead waved to and from in the just discernible breezes. He cast his cloak onto the rough green-brown grasses, sprawled his long frame on it as he picked up a few recently-fallen dates, rinsed them and, beginning to chew them, continued,

"It is a word that has come to mean much to me also. Its meaning has come home to me as I've observed his actions and behavior toward us. Surely, he has dealt so with no other nation! I think of the water and the manna and the Cloud of his Presence; and the awareness I have of his relentless, faithful attachment to us and indeed, of his patience with us . . . oh, and the patience with our forgetfulness and waywardness! Blessed be the name of Yahweh!" Their thoughts were often one and on this occasion seemed inseparable as Moshe again took up the thread,

"For in loving us he is determined to bring us to a place no other people have enjoyed; mind you, not because he does not love them, nor because we are more righteous than they.[2] No, but because he has determined that the best way to show it is through a people; indeed, I think, The People, becoming known as his sons—and indeed, collectively as his son![3] This makes his khesed visible and touchable . . . on the ground . . . accessible! You know, he once said to me, 'the word is very near you . . . not away in heaven so you can't reach it . . . nor across the sea so it's difficult to get to. No, my word is very near you; it's in your mouth and in your heart so that you *can* do it.'[4] And in the same way, he will make his life and his instructions accessible to all—through us! His desire is that the Goyim—all the 'other' peoples, see how it works as they see us! O, Yahweh, let it be!"

Yeshua expressed agreement with a strong, "ah-meen." The shadow in which they reclined was now solid as the sun had moved and the breeze had died. Nearby, water from a small spring gently pulsated and sang over grey, flat rock, washed of sand by the overflowing water. It was an idyllic place. It was now the heat of the

2. Deuteronomy 9:4–5 (cf. Titus 3:5)

3. Exodus 4:22 'my firstborn son' and Hosea 11:1

4. Deuteronomy 30:11–14 (Cf. Romans 10:8)

day and no-one was at the spring. The morning breeze as I said, had given way to mid-day stillness and there was no sound save the occasional cooing of the grey doves somewhere above in the denseness. Moshe loved to come here during the day. The bustle and sound of the camp was a comfortable distance to the west and separated from the wadi and spring by a low dune.

It was just to the east of Pisgah from whence he had glimpsed the great land into which Yahweh was to take Yeshua and the people. A moment of chagrin stole over him as he thought of the prospect, but he did not allow what is called among you, bitterness, to take hold. Instead he was reflective and thankful.

The Place

"I will soon go the way of all flesh," Moshe's dreamy, warmth-induced reverie had ended with the taking of a refreshing drink of water offered by Yeshua from a beautifully adorned skin he often carried over one shoulder. Yeshua also drank and said, "Father, what instructions have you?"

Moshe had already talked with him about The Place and its importance to Yahweh and the people and so he continued in this way;

"We are to be different, Yeshua. We are called to be different—difference is the essence of our call. Just as he has other-ness that separates him—and yet he is still accessible, so we too are to display other-ness, yet not across an unbridgeable divide. There is nothing more pleasing to the heart of Yahweh than that we, The People, are winsomely distinguished from the peoples of counterfeit gods. Oh, what an onus this places on us, but what a privilege too—for you have heard all the promises of the blessings that accompany his way. These blessings are exactly what makes self-evident the rightness of his way; they will cause some among the peoples to see—and will cause him to be the desire of nations! We are The People for this very purpose. He will not leave himself without a witness to his presence and nature. Yes, I remember when he first called me and said that His presence if you please,

59

would go with me—and with us—and would give a sense of ease within.[5] And we have seen that presence in the holy place and in the cloud and in the fire, not to mention in all his marvelous provision for us—and when you come into the land, his presence is then to be permanently in The Place, where he will reside; as he has said, 'you must seek The Place.'"[6]

Moshe spoke with an awe and conviction which he prayed Yeshua would carry into the land; for, as I Shaqaad had perceived, the actual land itself was to become a display of his blessing. Yes, the land was to be its affirmation and The People its embodiment!

Moshe spoke again, "Do you see it Yeshua? His heart is for nothing less than restoration of what was lost at the beginning; that partnership and accord with him that results in shalom and bounty and certainty." Yeshua did not need to respond; Moshe knew that he had it in his heart.

"Come Yeshua, shortly I will tell you about the white stones. They will stand as reminders and warnings at the gateway."

"The white stones? The gateway?"

"Yes, to the wonderful land you are to possess!"

Yeshua's heart was now full of anticipation, but he sensed that the great leader would divulge more in his own time.

---

5. Exodus 33:14 Note: the Hebrew word is NUACH

6. Deuteronomy 12:5,11,14,18,21 and etc. See this author's book, 'THE PLACE HaMakom; where Jerusalem's temples stood'

CHAPTER 10

Grandson of Ahron!

*They **joined themselves** also to Baal of Peor....*
And the plague broke out among them.
Then Phinehas stood up and intervened and
the plague was stopped.

(Psalm 106:30 NKJV **emphasis** added;
see Numbers 25 NKJV)

BUT, DEAR HUMAN READER, I am to keep you in a state of what you call anticipation about the stones and the gateway for it is fitting that you see and understand my point about the differences between those known as benei ha Elohim and those who choose to remain benei adam! Whilst there are many instances throughout your time, it is clear to me, that with you, a pattern in your behavior has emerged. It is one of drawing near to Yahweh Elohim when difficulties arise, only to rely on your own devices once again after he has very graciously answered your desperation! This too is an unknown for us, yet I see that it is, if you like, a consequence of having created a being with freedom to choose; we see that it was at great risk that he chose to do this—it is part and parcel (as you say) of being made analogous to him; in his image! We are not able to see why he did this, though we are beginning to see what it means to his whole being when you choose him and his way. We see that choice, each time you make it, somehow causes you to be made ever more into his likeness! We are conscious as sentient beings of the flow of life and favor that travels from him to you,

61

whenever that choice is made! May I use that wonderful word of yours . . . hallelu-Yah?

There was an incident in the plains of Moawb that illustrates my point and speaks of the weakness of some in succumbing to seduction—and the strength of others who are vigilant against it—and are zealous for Yahweh. I will invite one of the main characters to relate his experience. I have watched this man and indeed I was instructed to assist his endeavors. His name is Pinechas and he is the grandson of the great priest Ahron. He it is who now addresses you . . .

"How thankful I am for my heritage even though a great part of my life has been the wandering. But oh, I know the hearts of my grandfather and of my dear father, the priest El'eazar—not to mention the heart of our great one, Moshe who has led us all these years as we await entry into the land! I suppose some might see me as privileged, living as close as I do to those commissioned to safeguard the spiritual welfare of The People chosen by Yahweh as exemplars of his Name. And it is true that I've lived close to those who have been given great responsibility, and yes, close enough also to see and hear their frailties too! But I have seen the goodness of Yahweh and I have sought him and it has pained me deeply, as it does my father and many others when I saw again the rebellion and flagrant disobedience as some of our men recently gave way to base lusts with the women of Midiyan.

"In the days before the Deluge, some of the benei ha Elohim lusted after women who walked in the ways of the benei adam,[1] with disastrous results; that was when Yahweh said, 'I won't put up with this', and limited our lifespan. Now, similarly, in our day, what could not be achieved by Balaam, that prophet of falsehood trying to bring cursing upon us[2] has been achieved through seduction. Balaam could not turn Yahweh from his people, but the women of Moawb have succeeded in turning the people—yes, The People, from Yahweh![3] This they did, by the simple expediency of what

---

1. Genesis 6:1–3

2. Numbers chapters 22–24

3. Numbers 25 (note Hebrew Ha Am in v.1, 'The People began to commit

seemed like a harmless invitation to observe their manufactured gods and their acts of devotion! Why do so few guard and separate their hearts and minds? People who have seen over and again the merciful kindness of Yahweh, not to mention the folly of departure. What I have found is that the more I seek Yahweh, the more I understand how he must feel about the people's frequent easy and un-resisted drift into corrupted ways. And the more avidly I seek him, the more evident is the stark contrast between the beautiful, shining, rewarding ways of Yahweh and the dark and heavy pall over the Goyim, the benei adam, who've chosen their own paths and other idols! And now . . . ?

"A plague has again broken out among us and many are dying. Do they not see the connection between their rebellion and its fruit? What is wrong with their hearts? What kind of blindness is it that is unable to discern that the product of such provocative disobedience is inevitably both mortal and spiritual suicide? The physical plague that has broken out appears but a manifestation of that plague of the heart that is ever willing to tempt Yahweh. Once the heart becomes corrupted like this, that which is within becomes manifest without. It is a frightful thing. Do they believe that perhaps he will overlook lustful and unfaithful behavior!

Anyway, when I saw that man Zimri, one of our clan leaders consorting and cavorting with the woman Cozbi of Midiyan, I believe the very Spirit of Yahweh and his righteous zeal arose within me and I made a stand as Moshe had urged us to do. I too was aroused, but not in the flesh as they were, but in the spirit for I could see the damage they and those like them were doing to the entire company of benei ha Elohim, many of whom wept before the tent of meeting. For this man, Zimri, did this brazenly before them all, not to mention before Yahweh himself! I followed them both into the brothel tent they had made for their debaucheries and pinned them both to the ground as one (for they had become one), with my javelin. To the amazement of many, the plague stopped and was lifted from us. It is so clear that as soon as we weaken and compromise to join with the benei adam, we become one with

_____

harlotry')

their darkness[4] and begin to receive its fruit. We cannot be one with both Light and Darkness; they do not abide together. It must be the one or the other and it is we who must always make the choice. It is how we become and remain benei ha Elohim! Praised be Yahweh! Long live the visible difference! Moshe has heard from Yahweh and told me that he, Yahweh, has granted to me, Pinechas, grandson of the one known as The Mountain Range, The Lofty One (yes Ahron),[5] a covenant of shalom and of the priesthood![6] With such a heritage, how could I not stand up?

4. Psalm 106:28–31; Nu 25:3 where the Hebrew word TSAMAD means to join or bind to.

5. Ahron or Aaron means in Hebrew, Lofty or High Mountain or Mountain range.

6. Numbers 25:10–13

CHAPTER 11

Because of their wickedness!

It is not because of your righteousness or the uprightness of your heart that you go in to possess their land, but because of the wickedness of these nations that the LORD your God drives them out from before you (Deuteronomy 9:5 NKJV)

*Then Moses and the priests, the Levites, spoke to all Israel, saying, "Take heed and listen, O Israel: This day you have become **the people** of the Lord your God . . . "* (Deuteronomy 27:9 NKJV, Hebrew ha Am, the people, **emphasis** added)

And if it seems evil to you to serve the LORD, choose for yourselves this day whom you will serve, whether the gods which your fathers served that were on the other side of the River, or the gods of the Amorites, in whose land you dwell. But as for me and my house, we will serve the LORD (Joshua 24:15 NKJV)

Of mountains and lime-washed stones

READER, LET ME NOW resume. I left you a short time ago to let you hear from Pinechas and I'm sure what he had to say has helped you see with greater clarity, the difference between the two streams now flowing through time as your history unfolds. We digressed just when Moshe was about to tell Yeshua about the lime-washed stones and what he called the gateway to the land. Let me now continue with what I witnessed.

Yeshua hastened to the aging man's side, for even though he'd walked with him and been his constant attendant all these years and knew his every little habit and his gestures, mannerisms and foibles—yes, even though he knew these, yet he had the deepest respect and affection for Moshe—particularly for his wisdom and the way in which Yahweh was central to all that Moshe did and said. There had been an urgency in Moshe's call to both Yeshua and the other elders. It was late in the day and the occasion seemed to be of some importance for Moshe had made special preparations and a feast of good food. It was well past the defeat of the Amorite king Sichon and of Kheshbon and Og of B'shan and good food was available to the tribes. The men arrived in good spirits, conversations and laughter over the day's events bouncing around between them. The evening was soft with a mauve sky in the west and few clouds. The camp was quietening down, the voices of children heard here and there in laughter or tears as mothers took them through the end-of-day routines of washing and preparing for meals and bed. The air was balmy and still as the first stars now poked through the dimming canopy above, becoming brighter by the moment. As the men entered the copious tent of Moshe, the disturbance made the lamps misbehave in flickers that threw shadows up and down the walls and onto the expectant faces. Moshe greeted them each warmly with a double cheek-kiss. He loved these men with a love that came from Adonai. What flowed between them could, sometimes, almost make me desire to be human. But then I remembered the glorious flow that existed between beings of our type and indeed with the one you call Yahweh. It cannot be described here.

Moshe spoke to the gathering of the recent triumph Adonai had given them over Sichon and Og who had tried to hinder their progress and had acted so confrontationally toward them, and Moshe reminded them to be ever thankful to Yahweh. They all recounted at some length their recent memories of B'lak the king of Amori who had hired that twisted mercenary, Balaam to bring a curse on Ysra-El, and they chuckled at his embarrassment at being able only to bless The People upon whom Yahweh had spoken favor and of how Balaam's ass was the only one who could get through to him! They roared with glee over that. They spoke then of how he had given the land east of River Yarden to Reuven and Gad and one half of the Menash-sheh tribe, because they had desired that portion for their livestock.

"I have given it to them—and Menash-sheh's other half will be on the other side of Yarden—because they have agreed to come across Yarden to assist in the warfare that will be involved taking the land west of Yarden." There was general head shaking of agreement around the room and the usual ensuing discussion enjoyed by men of the east about Moshe's action and its ramifications and how Reuven and Gad and Menash-sheh would be held to their word. Outside, a plethora of desert moths, small and large swarmed around the slivers of light coming through a slot where the door covering had not been fully closed. As well, a few teenaged youths tried, without getting too close, to hear the discussion within. Apart from distinguishing an occasional word, they heard only a muffled rise and fall of converse and sometimes laughter through the heavy skin coverings. By and by they made their way back to their family's tents. In a pause in the discussion, it was Yeshua who spoke:

"Father, you must tell me about the stones and the altar you mentioned some time ago."

"Aha, yes—the lime-washed stones. I am pleased you remembered. Listen my son Yeshua—and bear witness, all of you." Moshe began quietly, "You remember how you and K'leb spoke of the Vale of Sh'kem with a prominence on either side? On the north, the one they call Har Eival and on the south Har Griziym?"[1] Yeshua remembered what he had seen.

The narrow gateway to life

"They," intoned the great man lifting his voice a fraction of a decibel, "form a kind of representative gateway within the great land,

---

1. Known to the reader as Ebal and Gerizim, see Deuteronomy 27

They are to the north and west of the place where you will cross Yarden and they stand near the middle of the land, and, most importantly. . ." Moshe paused and, to ensure he had Yeshua and the company's full attention, for by now the hour was late and the food well eaten, tapped his grand old staff on the ground—yes, the very one that he had stretched over Yam Suph and with which he had hastily smitten the rock at K'desh: "It is at Sh'kem, there between Har Eival and Har Griziym that our fathers Ivrahim and Yaakov[2] long ago made sacrifice. Do you see, dear Yeshua, that you and the people are to know that in being there, you are following in the very footsteps of these great fathers and that your walk is to be one of trust like theirs? You are to take some significant stones and plaster then with a heavy lime-wash and on them write again the words of the covenant of Yahweh."

Yeshua's eyes brightened with the dawning of this revelation and he clapped his hands together and smiled with delight, his teeth suddenly appearing above his salt and pepper beard as he let out a spontaneous, "hallelu-Yah!" A murmur of curious approval waved around the assembly like barley in the breeze. Moshe knew he had their attention and then Yeshua added his own further revelation, "And the stones on the mountain with Yahweh's words will also be a reminder of Sinay . . . . Surely it's like a new beginning!"

"Yes" continues Moshe, "a new start indeed; I would love to be there, but it is not to be. Yahweh desires that The People pass between those mountains and there hear again the word of his covenant. And, Yeshua—you are to build on Har Eival an altar and make sacrifice to him, and the altar must be of uncut stones—stones that are shalem![3] But, more than that—for you are to make Har Eival represent the displeasure of Yahweh when we go the way of the benei adam and Griziym will represent his favor when we act as benei ha Elohim."

One of the elders who had been listening intently cleared his throat and spoke up with, "but surely it's the river, the Yarden

---

2. Genesis 12:7 and 33:18–20

3. The word used in Deuteronomy 27:6 and Joshua 8:31 is shalem meaning whole, sound, having integrity, (from which shalom derives)

that forms the gateway to the land?" To which Moshe responded with a smile,

"It is the break . . . the river signifies the end of the wanderings—very much as Yam Suph separated us from Egypt, so Yarden will separate you from the wanderings of unbelief and alienation, and into readiness to move forward freely and to possess your destiny. Yarden will be like the closing of a door on one season, and remember, there must also be circumcision then for those males not yet circumcised. But Griziym and Eival will represent the acceptance of, and agreement to the house rules of your new possession. Yarden closes the old; Sh'kem is the official opening of the new!

"It's a gateway because it's an act of renewal of covenant; of re-constitution as The People known as Yahweh's. Written on those special stones at that gateway will be the words he gave you to live by so long ago! You will, as it were, immerse yourselves in them in passing between them and you will recite in the hearing of all,[4] the promised blessings of obedience and the consequences of disobedience. The People must respond with a loud ah-meen of agreement! In hearing Yahweh's word and agreeing to proceed, they will become committed to it and to him, understanding the terms of the covenant by which life comes. As you are very aware, his word is the gateway to life and health and prosperity; as Yahweh has said, they are the words of life; they are the words that provide choice—to do or to ignore. These words and this action will be that significant. They will again set you apart as benei ha Elohim, so that you will be, as Yahweh desires, a testimony to the nations."

Moshe reclined comfortably on some favorite cushions and took a long draft of water while the import of what he had instructed sank into, in profound silence, the assembled hearts.

"Let me explain how it will work. You are to take uncut stones and plaster them with lime plaster in which the words of the

---

4. Deuteronomy 27:4 26 and Joshua 8:30–35. It should be noted that the natural amphitheater formed by the faces of the two hills at this point provided acoustic assistance to the reading of the blessings and curses. This phenomenon has been tested on numerous occasions.

testimony are to be engraved. One of the first things you must do is remind the people that it is always about choosing; their choice. Death or life, sickness or health, defeat or victory, confusion or shalom; to become benei ha Elohim or benei adam! And— one of the reasons for The Place and its importance among you is that it may serve as a constant reminder to choose Yahweh Elohim! Anyway, as I've said, let the blessing be on Har Griziym and the curse be on Har Eival.[5] They represent the nature of our Yahweh toward our behavior—for it is judgment or grace, judgment or grace . . . and he will decide when the time is right for each. All are to see how our beloved Yahweh always desires to make it clear by demonstration with things that we know and recognize, that there is a choice; and that it is ours to make—and that our choices have consequences. It reminds me of the choice in Edhen and the two trees—one of life and the other of death; blessing and cursing. For that is how he defines a people for himself!"

Yeshua broke in with a comment: "Aba," he began, "the river Yarden is the boundary between old unbelief and new belief, leading into the nuach[6] he has promised. Our past has been marked by restless-ness but our future lies across that divide and the river will serve as the transition from restlessness to restfulness; and Sh'kem will remind how to maintain and live within the restfulness. In these we become, as he has said through you, separated as The People of Yahweh!" Yeshua had a heart awake to spiritual truth and his words brought a resounding "ahmeen" from the lips of Moshe who then continued,

"I want to declare this to all the people. Call an assembly for the day after tomorrow and I shall address them one and all about these matters."

And so, they dismissed, happy with anticipation, into the night with its resplendent canopy of a million lights above them, and it struck Yeshua that Yahweh had his lights above—and here, on the eastern shores of Yarden, millions of his lights below. His

---

5. Deuteronomy 11:29
6. Exodus 33;14; Deuteronomy 12:9; 25:19; Joshua 1:13

silent prayer into that sky was, "Yahweh, let us be as those lights above, to all the benei adam."

So, I The Watcher known as Shaqaad, beheld as the people assembled and were addressed by the great Moshe with the priests—and, as your annals show, in prophetic anticipation, here is what he said:

"Be silent and listen, O Ysra-El: This day you have become *The People* of Yahweh Eloha. You shall therefore obey the voice of Yahweh Eloha, and observe his commandments and his statutes which I command you today. These tribes shall stand on Har Griziym to bless the people when you've crossed over Yarden—Shymown, Levi, Yudah, Yissaskar, Yosef, and Binyamin. And these shall stand on Har Eival to curse: Reuven, Gad, Assher, Zevulun, Dan, and Naftawli."[7]

Then the Levites continued to outline in detail—while the people paid serious attention (for they too sensed that they were on the verge of a new thing)—all the curses and the blessings. But oh, the promises for continuing as benei ha Elohim were extraordinary and I could see in them the heart of Yahweh Elohim for The People. For the blessings included the fruit of wombs and livestock and produce as well as protection from those who have evil intent toward The People. Nothing was left lacking: barns, handiwork, rains in season, all kinds of prosperity and shalom.[8] And, the crowning glory? Why, it revealed the whole purpose, for here is what the Levites told: "Yahweh will establish you as his qodesh people and then all the peoples of earth will observe that you are called by the name of Yahweh and hold you in awe!"[9]

I myself, Shaqaad, watched in awe and appreciation of Yahweh's plan. I could see that the people saw the truth and understood that they would require the thing you call faith—and at that time at least, knew that it would come as they chose the good path.

7. Deuteronomy 27:12–13
8. Deuteronomy 28:1–14
9. Deuteronomy 28:10

71

Part Four: **In the Land of the benei ha Elohim**

CHAPTER 12

Distinctive . . . or just the same?

*. . . that we . . . . may be **distinct from** all the other people who are upon the face of the earth* (Exodus 33:16 NASB and author's translation, **emphasis** added)

*. . . that we also **may be like** all the nations, and that our king may judge us and go out before us and fight our battles* (1 Samuel 8:5, 20 NKJV **emphasis** added)

"But why is it that the people ask for a king?" The questioner was an attendant of the great Shemuel, last of the judges and first of the prophets of The People. The servant, Eliphas, sat at a crude table in the home of Shemuel in the settlement known as Ramah near the hill country of Ephrayim. Eliphas seemed more than puzzled; indeed, he was perplexed for he knew well the desire of Yahweh's heart for a distinctive people.

"Ah", says Shemuel, a look of resignation written across his handsome features and a tone of acceptance in his textured voice, "You are justified in being perplexed Eliphas, for I too know the heart of Yahweh in this matter. It is not that a ruler is necessarily a bad thing—no, but it is the motive of The People that displeases Yahweh. For their motive is to be as like to the Goyim as possible rather than be different, and as like Yahweh as possible! This means they have forgotten His heart; they have missed again the message and their purpose, listening only to their own fancies." Shemuel looked out on the sere, rock-strewn hills toward Shiloh where the Tabernacle stood and reflected disappointedly on the wayward barren-ness of his own sons who also, as so many, walked according to their bellies and typified the spirit of the age. They were a source of constant shame to him but he had learned to commit them over to Yahweh. Of course, he also felt keenly the rejection of his own leadership implied in the people's request; indeed, it was almost a demand. He faced the familiar and trusted eyes of Eliphas as he continued, "indeed, he has shown me that it is not me they have rejected but Yahweh himself, because what they are really doing is failing to trust and wait for his choosing and appointment. Waiting with patience is so much a part of what Yahweh always desires for each of us, for waiting is the evidence of trust. A king they will have . . . oh yes—but he will be but a reflection of their own desires and hearts, not of his. A king, not so much like the nations, but like themselves! I do not think it will end well. Indeed, I feel—no—it is more than a feeling; he has instructed me that I must warn The People what life will be like under the king they call for.[1] For he will be a harsh shepherd and taskmaster; he will be a taker and not a giver. My heart grieves, but Yahweh has said to heed their voice and give them a king!"

Dear reader, it is a painful story with which I will not burden you, of how the king whom the people lusted for, was indeed too much like them and became self-serving and a snare to them. What Yahweh had in mind was a king like himself—and, as your writings disclose, he did find one after his own heart,[2] who blessed The People. The final straw for Sha'ul was when he rebelled against Yahweh's command in the incident of the offering,[3] but as I said, I will not burden you and, time is short.

---

1. 1 Samuel 8:9–19
2. 1 Samuel 13:14 and Acts 13:22
3. 1 Samuel 15, especially vv.22–25

CHAPTER 13

Showdown and return to apart-ness

*How long will you falter between two opinions? If the
LORD is God, follow Him; but if Baal, follow him.* (1 Kings
18:21 NKJV)

IT WAS UNCONSTRAINED FRENZY—AN orgy of wild and wilder
desperation. Such human behavior is mysterious to our kind; I
can but tell what was observed. Blood gushed about from veins
and arteries; a repugnant scene. The blood was that of frantic men,
calling upon a god who neither heard nor cared; and the longer he
neither heard nor cared the more desperate became the effort to
have him hear and care. As though he'd be persuaded by the self-
harm of those held in his thrall. We see that such passions in the
humans is a product linked directly to the independence of those
known as benei adam. Not that it is never seen in the benei ha
Elohim, but there it is usually recognized for what it signals, and
departed from with the action known as repentance—the change
of direction resulting from a mind set on qodesh.

The frenetic and horrifying tempo and noise rose unabated
from the hilltop throughout the day. Making matters even more
bizarre was the taunt of the man of God;

"You need to yell louder! After all, he's a god; perhaps he's
dealing with a complaint; or maybe he's gone to relieve himself—
or maybe on a road trip or taking a nap and can't quite hear you."

I, the Watcher Shaqaad tell you, it made matters even more
bizarre because the response of the four hundred shamans was

indeed to shout and scream more loudly and to pitch themselves more demonically into their tormented delirium to the point of collapse! The scene could be viewed as both tragic yet weirdly comic. Comic in its futility; tragic because so much was at stake for the now hysterical and near spent, four hundred. The called-for fire to consume the offering failed to materialize. In starkest contrast to the exhausted subjects, the god was mockingly silent and indifferent; the great purported son of El and Aserah, the one known in Kna'an as Ba'al, made no response, remained unimpressed—showed no mercy. No fire came. It was time for the god who had neither power to act, nor love for those held within its thrall, to be exposed as bogus and without claim to obeisance; time for eyes of unbelief to be opened; time to shame those who had been led captive by the subtlety of lies and images and persuasions of fools and demons.

Time indeed for hearts which should have known much better, to repent of spiritual adultery and its resulting offence to Yahweh. And time to see that rain and prosperity and well–being and protection and success were part and parcel of the package of life in partnership with Yahweh, the only God who loves!

And so, your great prophet Eliyyah—he whose name means my God is Yahweh—in the magnificent confidence of that thing both Yahweh and you call faith, stepped forward. It was he who had challenged the priests of Ba'al and Aserah to the showdown and had mocked them in their craven folly. And so assured was Eliyyah that he erected an altar to Yahweh with twelve stones (to represent the completeness of Ysra-El), with a trench all around it which he then commanded, with its sacrifice, to be drenched again and again with water—the commodity you most desperately needed in this terrible drought—until saturated!

Then he called on our great Yahweh to demonstrate his presence and power so that the hearts of you who were called the benei ha Elohim, might be corrected and turned. And oh, how the fire fell from above—and with such intensity that it consumed all of the offering, the wood and even the twelve stones of that altar! What a day it was in the annals of your people—The

People. And what a repentance ensued and what a slaughtering of the evil, deceived and deceiving prophets of Ba'al! You and I saw how jealous our Yahweh is for The People he chose as his demonstration—and then . . . ? We saw the much-needed rain for which Eliyyah had prayed. The awful drought had so evidently been a product of your failure to be separated from evil and to be the wholehearted benei ha Elohim.

CHAPTER 14

Wherein Dawid muses on Apart-ness and Power

When Ysra-El went out of Egypt . . . . Judah became His **apart-ness** *(hallowing) and Israel His* **power** (Psalm 114:2 see Wycliffe's Translation, Jubilee Bible, GOD'S WORD Translation, **emphasis** and parenthesis added)

BEFORE I, SHAQAAD, ALLOW that shepherd boy who became king—your great Dawid—to share with you some of his musings, let me bring an instruction to assist your understanding. We Watchers are also known as qodesh, or 'holy ones.' We understand what qodesh means and we are part and parcel of his holy other-ness. Around his throne, we all cry, 'qodesh'! We recognize it as his chief characteristic, from which flows his every other attribute! His khane–grace flows from his holiness; he is merciful because he is first and foremost, holy; he keeps his word because he is holy. The first of you, 'Dam, was, like us, holy because he came forth from the qodesh One—Elohim; was joined to him. 'Dam's decision to participate with Chaveh in that which Elohim had forbidden, immediately severed them from him, and hence from his other-ness. Since *that* moment, the invitation has always been to come back to it—to re-join Elohim. We observe that when any one of you does so, the dark membrane which has separated you from him, vanishes and you become one with him! Then, the new relationship becomes one that simply requires maintenance on your part. I say, simply, because it is not complicated—though for some it seems hard. But its simplicity is in the fact that it is just an ongoing exercise of will; you simply must choose, yes, as your time unfolds before you, to go with him and his plan. Day to day; moment to moment. We have observed that for those who succeed at it, it has become a matter of practice and, little by little, it appears to become almost impossible for them to make any other choice! We have noticed that this choosing is quite often tested and yet, as those who are determined, make the choice, they become entrusted with a greater flow of all the things that reside with him and flow from him, to them! I hope I am making this understandable for we can see that it results in ever increasing fruitfulness for those who practice it.

In the portion you see above from your Psalm 114, it is clear from the Hebrew language that our Yahweh expressed something about himself through The People. In the exodus and through the sea they became separated and special. By the election and purpose of Yahweh these people, in a mysterious sense, became *his* 'apart-ness' (that is, his qodesh holiness) and his power, made visible in the earth! I see that the Targum (the Aramaic paraphrase of the Hebrew Bible) says it this way—*'the congregation of the house of Yudah was united to his holiness, and Ysra-El to his power.'*

In other words, to see them was to see the apart–ness and the very power of Yahweh—and that was what he intended. That's why the Psalm continues, explaining how your natural world 'saw' it and reacted; "the sea saw it and fled; Yardan turned back. The mountains skipped like rams, the little hills like lambs." It reveals that it was your presence that was the *actual* presence of the Lord![1]

So . . . here is Dawid, musing further on this marvel . . .

I have seen it; I have seen it! Yes, I Dawid, because he has revealed it to my heart—that farthest-in part of my being, so that I know it as only things that he makes known can be known. For those things are known by a distinctive and indelible impression on the inside. It's a knowing that abides and which nothing can shake or dislodge. I praise him for it! For what I have seen is that his farthest-in desire is that we be one with him—functionally and demonstrably—that his 'apart-ness' (qodesh) becomes our apart-ness; that his is seen via ours. And what is it that we are apart from? Those actions, deeds and

1. Psalm 114:7

habits from which he is apart. Yes, apart from all falsehood including invented gods; separate from self-seeking, self-aggrandizement, self-power; The People who rely on and put all our weight down upon what he says and promises. And yes—separate from those I and all before me know as benei adam; not in a conceited way, but as those who cannot join with practices with which he cannot join. My writings and those of others have often reflected this; we stand as benei ha Elohim, they as benei adam . . . I remember writing 'my soul is among lions; I lie among the benei adam who are set on fire, whose teeth are spears and arrows and their tongue a sharp sword.'² And again, I recall saying something like, 'do you speak righteousness; do you judge uprightly, you benei adam?'³ So, as I muse and meditate on this, I see so evidently how he desires us to be inextricably joined in showing the beauty and benefit of his apart-ness to all so that they too may come and enjoy him, and it! In that sense, when he took us out of Mitsrayim it was for this purpose—that we become his apart-ness. Yes, I have written it thus in the songs he has given me; 'Yudah became his apart-ness and Ysra-El His power.'⁴

Yes, he called us to be different. Just as I have written, 'the heavens declare the glory of El and the expanse proclaims his handwork'⁵ so we too are a work of his hands that declares and proclaims his government and its product, shalom. And—not only to be his apart-ness exemplified, but also to be his power, made visible. I cannot forget when I stood before Goliat, that Gittite freak—that fleshly representation of all the powers arrayed against our Yahweh! For it was with a stone from my shepherd's sling that the giant was diminished and fell. Oh—yes, and Yahweh had me take five stones from the brook for were there not five lords of Pelehsheth?⁶ I praise Yahweh, for but one stone was needed. Yes, I have learned where his power resides on earth; it resides right there, in our apart-ness.

2. Psalm 57:4. See also Psalm 12:1 & 8, 'the wicked prowl on every side when vileness is exalted among the benei adam.'

3. Psalm 58:1

4. See Psalm 114 above

5. Psalm 19

6. Philistia

It is ours that keeps us joined to his! As soon as we join any other we become separated from the power. He is a jealous God indeed and knows what benefits us and what harms us. This is his khesed[7] loyalty. I believe I sense a song coming on—

> *Because your khesed is better than life,*
> *my lips shall praise you.*
> *Thus, I will bless you while I live;*
> *I will lift up my hands in your name[8]*

I have also come to realize that the 'other' things to which we join ourselves are sometimes the very things with which he has blessed us! He would have us hold the blessings he sends as precious and yet as no substitute for himself and his presence and his power. If we are to remain the representation of his apart-ness and power, we must ever guard our hearts to ensure that we are becoming more like him as benei ha Elohim and less like the benei adam[9] with whom we are surrounded. It is not only the prophets that Yahweh uses to bring correction to The People: he has talked to me about my son, Shalomoh, who is to build the great Bayth-El—the House of God that he has put in my heart. Yahweh has said that if Shalomoh goes astray, he will reprove him with the blows of the benei adam![10]

---

7. Khesed means relentless covenant loyalty

8. See Psalm 63:3–4

9. For further examples of the use of benei adam see Eccl. 2:8 & 3.18, Micah 5:7 and Isaiah 52:14

10. 2 Samuel 7:14 NKJV and Hebrew Bible

CHAPTER 15

'If my people . . . .'

AH, WE MUST HURRY on. I told you at the start—when I told you about Mitsrayim—that the story was a long one and now, after I have told you about the great Shalomoh, I will compress it because we must get to the great culmination. For the story has a culmination, because everything that Elohim does has, in your time-terms, a beginning, a passage—and an end!

The City of Dawid had never seen anything like this. The dedication of the temple built by Shalomoh had been glorious, accompanied as it was by the music and the praise and celebration that embraced all and continued for days, centered as it was upon the Bayth-El[1] and more particularly, upon Yahweh Adonai whose fiery presence fell there on Dedication Day![2] Your priests could not enter the Bayth-El because of the Presence! And then there was the Bayth-El itself, that most beautiful place—indeed, right above The Place at Gikhon, spoken of and visited and named by your fathers as HaMakom. No wonder Adonai visited you that day, for it was the fulfillment of what your father Yaakov had said so long ago, "how fear–inducing is The Place (HaMakom); this is none other than the Bayth-El—House of God—the very gateway to heaven!"[3] And then the great Shalomoh spoke to all of you, of how Yahweh appeared to him at night and called you his people and reminded him of his covenant faithfulness to you. Your scribes

1. Bayth-El (Bethel) means House of God, built at Ha Makom (The Place). See this author's book of that name.

2. 2 Chronicles 7:1–3

3. Genesis 28:17 (Scripture4all and Author's translation)

have recorded it and here is some of what the great Yahweh said . . . and then I will tell you of the event I started out to tell you about, in just a moment: 'When I shut up heaven and there is no rain, or command the locusts to devour the land, or send pestilence among my people— if my people who are called by my name will humble themselves, and pray and seek my face, and turn from their wicked ways, then I will hear from heaven, and will forgive their sin and heal their land. Now my eyes will be open and my ears attentive to prayer made in this place.'[4]

And you, whom he called 'my people'—and known throughout your annals as Ha Am—The People, were yet to see more extraordinary things! As I said, the building and then the dedication of the Bayth-El was extraordinary, even to my sight, but then came the procession of kings and queens to behold what Yahweh had done and to hear the wisdom of Shalomoh.[5] Why, it was just as Elohim had said through the great Moshe, "I will set you high above all nations I have made, in praise and name and recognition!"[6] In speaking of the wisdom of Shalomoh, I must remind you of how he saw and spoke of Wisdom as a person, calling to all the benei adam to come over and receive her riches.[7] It was an invitation to become part of the benei ha Elohim! But the one that all your people remember is the arrival of royalty from the kingdom of the people of Saba in the person of their queen![8]

I, Shaqaad, who have seen glory that is beyond anything in your realm—saw beauty and honor of a kind different to ours, yet, I must say, extraordinary. For the City of Dawid could not contain her lavish retinue and the animals and gifts of spices and

4. 2 Chronicles 7:13-15. Note that 'this place' in v.15 is again, Ha Makom, See Footnote 1

5. 1 Kings 4:34

6. Deuteronomy 26:19

7. Proverbs 8 where verse 8 says, 'my voice is to the sons of men' (benei adam). David and Solomon used benei adam in Ecclesiastes 3:18, Psalm 31:19 and 145:12 to name a few. In Psalm 31:19 God stores up riches for those who love him, to display before the eyes of the sons of men (benei adam). 8. 2 Chronicles 9:1-12.

8. 2 Chronicles 9

gold objects and jewels, all as gifts for his majesty, Shalomoh. I can tell you that your whole city was in an uproar. You had heard for days of her coming and Shalomoh accommodated her in specially prepared rooms in the palace, but the Valley Chedron and the king's gardens were filled with tents and camels and caged birds and exotic animals. For many days, it provided both commerce and entertainment for young and old from Dawid's City! Ah, I saw that she was quite breathless with wonder as she congratulated Shalomoh and gave praise to your Yahweh.

And now—let me tell you briefly of the prophets sent by Yahweh in his khane and compassion for you, Ha Am, The People! For I perceive that he understood your weakness and frailty and raised them up among you—yes, even within both your camps—Yudah and Yaakov after your great division at the death of Shalomoh. Their purpose was to help you maintain your walk among the others as benei ha Elohim. It was a calling that you often made difficult for them in the extreme. Indeed, there were occasions when I thought that he would finish with you all! But he kept on calling forth prophets and bringing his warnings and encouragements through them. They were his mouthpiece for your good—not just for your survival, but so that you would prosper under his hand and thereby, continue to show the difference.

CHAPTER 16

A conversation overheard: Maintenance by Grace through the Seers

Since the day that your fathers came out of Egypt until this day, I have even sent you all my servants the prophets, daily rising up early and sending them (Jeremiah 7:25 NKJV)

And the LORD has sent to you all His servants the prophets, rising early and sending them, but you have not listened nor inclined your ear to hear (Jeremiah 25:4 NKJV)

. . . because they have not heeded My words, says the LORD, which I sent to them by My servants the prophets, rising up early and sending them; neither would you heed, says the LORD. . . (Jeremiah 29:19 NKJV)

I have sent you all my servants the prophets, rising early and sending them (Jeremiah 44:4 NKJV)

DEAR EARTHLY READER, KINDLY allow me the liberty of some explanation before I proceed with the story. I understand that there were three governmental roles Yahweh installed for the spiritual and civil government, correction and well-being of The People. The roles were those of King, Priest and Prophet. (As you will soon see, all these functions found their fulfilment in your One known as Messchiach). The role of the prophets (or seers) in the life of Ysra-El was to be as those who saw the big picture, saw you, Ha Am, The People, as you stood among the nations; saw the drifts and currents that could lead to loss of integrity and witness—and spoke to kings and people alike both the encouragement or correction of Yahweh, reminding you of consequences or coming corrections. Theirs was an awesome—not to mention, often thankless obligation, but then, so also was the obligation upon you, The People, to shine. Their presence among you spoke of the care and khane of Yahweh as your Shepherd.

Some of Ysra-El's great prophets were contemporaries, as were Ysha'yah and Hosheah. Ysha'yah was of courtly origins and lived in, and spoke to, your southern kingdom (Yudah) whilst Hosheah lived in and addressed his message to your northern kingdom. On one or two occasions their paths crossed and I want to share with you, or rather, have Ysha'yah describe their sojourn and conversation, during one of those occasions . . . .

"I have to say that I was completely undone by what he showed me in a vision. When I say he, of course I mean the One we call Adonai and Yahweh. . .and I saw him! Yes, I was spending time seeking his presence, worshiping . . .and there he was! Of course, I had always known that he was there—in The Place, in the Holy of Holies and between the wings of those kheruvim above the ark. But on this day, I saw him. Or rather, he chose to show himself to me. Adonai right there, on a throne, exalted and so majestic that I was emptied and reduced to abject and total inadequacy."

"Did Adonai speak?" Asked my compatriot, Hosheah from the northern kingdom, Shomaron (or Samaria as the reader will know it). My heart had been so delighted to greet him and I found him to be a man of intense gentleness and compassion who indeed had great khane from Yahweh upon him—even after all he'd been through!

"Oh yes indeed, he spoke!" I responded, "But let me try to tell of what I saw before he spoke. For it was majestic almost beyond the power of my words. The temple itself seemed to be filled with the train of his kingly robe that flowed down from a vast throne upon which Adonai was seated . . .and above the temple stood winged and glorious seraphim.[1] Even they, glorious

---

1. See Isaiah 6

creatures that they are, covered their faces with two wings and their feet with two wings and flew in the heavenly vault with two wings. And they covered their feet and their faces because of the terrifying otherness of Yahweh! And oh, the cry from their lips—at once paralyzing and yet strangely beautiful and beneficent! It comprised but one word, as though no other word would suffice . . .as though more would be sacrilege! The word was our word, that splendid word that describes who he is more than all words. . . 'qodesh.' Over and again the word seemed to be communicated, not to my ears but to my inmost self—my heart, 'qodesh, qodesh, qodesh . . . is Yahweh of army-hosts.' I can tell you that it wasn't just the doorposts that shook; my heart and whole being shook with them, for not only did I glimpse the Otherness; I saw also, at once, my own distant and repulsive darkness.

"I could neither rise nor speak except to cry my woe at the difference and distance I saw between his qodesh and my taintedness! And then, just when the horror of what I saw in myself and the uncleanness of my life and lips was about to engulf me in condemnation, what was this? One of the exalted seraphim creatures flew to me . . . and instead of terror, I was now infused with the profoundest sense of acceptance and embrace as he, with a coal taken from the holy altar of incense, touched it to my lips and said that my guiltiness was taken away and my sin, atoned for!"

My new-found compatriot, Hosheah was moved to tears and shook his head in wonder. He knew that what I was telling him was utterly true as he offered, after a long silence,

"Having revealed his qodesh otherness to you, did you know the reason for this mighty visitation?"

"Oh yes" I responded, "for then I heard, not the voices of the seraphim but that of Adonai himself asking whom he could send to The People with the revelation. Believe me I could not have refused had I desired to because my whole being was caught up in a sense of great destiny and purpose and knowing, so that I found words of consent rolling across my newly-cleansed lips, 'behold me; send me!' I was at once compelled and yet compliant; commanded and yet offering. I have never so sensed being caught up into the grand plan of all things in an understanding that seemed to be flowing from that throne that I saw. It was utter benevolence that enveloped me and I knew I was secure. Dear Hosheah, it has so gripped my being that I now feel his very heart for The People— and I'm to go with the message of his otherness even though he then said that the message will make their hearts dull as they hear without understanding."

"How long?" queried Hosheah.

"That was exactly my question of Adonai![2] To which he said it would be until cities are laid waste and the land is desolate . . . and yet, and yet, I was assured that there would be a remnant who stayed faithful. Oh, my friend, I have felt his heart and I will never be the same again. But come, I must show you where this took place and show you our city and let you feel also his heart–beat, although I sense you already have—and have much to share—I have heard a little of your ministry and I want to hear what he is saying to our northern brothers."

I gathered some nuts and dates into a small sack and a water skin which Hosheah obligingly carried over one shoulder, and led him out into the street. Our king, Uzziyah had been dead only a few months. Ah, he had been a good king and had long reigned, defeating attackers and building our cities and fortifications. At the end, some pride crept in, but by and large he was used greatly by Yahweh to bless The People. His son Yotham now reigns and he is something of an unknown. Sadly because of Uzziyah's folly at the end, The People have become loose and careless of the things of Yahweh. I shared these things with Hosheah and then added, "And the call of Yahweh to which I responded means, I know, that I will have to warn The People and declare the truth about where their drift will lead. But, my dear Hosheah" I further ventured, "I want to hear your story and of how the Qodesh One of Ysra-El[3] —for that is from henceforth how I will think and write of him—of how he has dealt with you and spoken to you for Ysra-El of the north."

---

2. Isaiah 6:11–13

3. Isaiah predominantly calls God, the holy one of Israel. He uses the name 27 times in the book bearing his name and once in 2 Kings 19:22

The day was balmy, but with a cool breeze from the north and east and the stones of Yerushalem shone under an autumn sun. We paused in a sun-drenched space against a south facing wall that protected us from the breeze. Hosheah, his red beard stark against his mostly white linen tunic, admired the city and its hustle and murmur, for everywhere he turned people were carrying and fetching and dealing in goods—or, like us, trading words, thoughts and ideas. We were near the locality known to The People as Tzion—where stood HaMakom (The Place), spoken of through the ages by Ivrahim and Yaakov and Dawid.[4] The Place was where that magnificent temple of the great Shalomoh now stood, high above that wonderful ever-flowing spring, Gikhon whose stream is known also as Shiloach and whose waters were forced upward by great underground pressure[5] and through pipes to meet the needs of the sacrifices and ceremonial washings. Hosheah had not yet visited the temple during this visit and I had promised to take him there, but for the moment we paused in this sunny spot and drank water as I waited for his response. I took the opportunity to also mention another thing Adonai had said, "He told me that both Ysra-El in the north and we, Yudah in the south have both, in calling on foreign kings for help, forsaken the gentleness of Shiloach.[6] You see, its flowing, 'living' water, represents the presence and the power of Yahweh right here with us, yes, right at Ha Makom . . . where we will be in a moment!" But now I really had to let Hosheah continue—

A harlot people

"Ah" says he, finally taking his rich, brown eyes off the bustle all around, "my story is different—and yet, so much the same, for I

4. See this author's book THE PLACE, published by Wipf & Stock, ISBN 9781532630422

5. Gihon is a karst spring, capable in those days of forcing water upward to significant heights.

6. See Isaiah 8:6

too have seen the drift away from that which would keep us wholly benei ha Elohim.

"While you, Ysha'yah, have been shown so wonderfully his qodesh otherness, and how far The People have drifted from it, what he has shown me is the pain he experiences over their unfaithfulness as they have become adulterers by embracing foreign gods!" His eyes filled and welled over and I knew that he was feeling what Yahweh feels and wondered how this had been revealed to him. And then he told me!

"As you know, while your king in the south has been Uzziyah, we in the north have been in a time of prosperity, this time with the second king with the name Yerovom, who at least was much better than the earlier Yerovom who split our kingdom, worshipped the Ba'als and killed the prophets! But alas, our story is much the same, for The People have drifted and, as Yahweh foretold, troubled times are coming. It is of great interest to me that he has chosen you to write and speak mainly to the south and me to the north—and our names are so similar, both different forms of Yeshua;[7] It is a demonstration of his heart, for salvation is the central truth from him! Salvation belongs to him even as our great king, Dawid has said.[8] It is who he is for it's his nature to rescue continually all who will put their weight down on what he says. I believe it is the continuous activity with which he is engaged on our behalf as we love Him."

I was moved to declare a loud "ah-meen," as Hosheah's gift for declaration was beginning to be displayed!

"But let me tell the story of Yahweh's pain, for I have felt it as I'm sure you have too. To illustrate it to them, he asked a very difficult thing of me, a man who longed to be loved of a woman. He asked me to take a wife from among the harlots—to rescue her from a life of destruction and shame, just as he had rescued us. And, only because his word to me was unmistakably clear, I found a dear woman, G'mer, and took her as my wife! You can imagine the impact this had on our community—and the talk that ensued.

---

7. The name Hosea means 'salvation' and Isaiah means 'Yahweh is salvation'

8. Psalm 3:8 NKJV

But they knew! They knew it was a picture. As you are so well aware, they watch the seers, even if just to criticize or self-justify. In their hearts they know our high calling.

"It was an unambiguous picture of Yahweh's action toward us in rescuing us to make us into a productive wife. And then the names by which I was to call the children of this woman, my wife, who kept straying and returning to past ways! After giving us a son I was instructed to name him Yizre'el because, whilst it sounds so like Ysra-El,[9] it actually means to be scattered by Yahweh! I can tell you that to name him so tragically brought no pleasure to my soul, but I knew that Yahweh desired to speak a living sermon to The People and so I counted it a privilege. It was to be a reminder that if there is no returning, Yahweh will scatter The People. The next child—and believe me, I know that The People, along with me, had to question the patrimony of them all—the next was a daughter to whom I was to give the name Lo Ruchamah[10] to remind everyone that Yahweh is running out of compassion for people whose hearts keep forsaking him. Through all these times I had to pursue G'mer, for whom Yahweh had given me much love and pity!"

For a moment Hosheah's pain became visible through the two dark windows below his brow and I could say nothing. I stood there, my back to the wall and alongside him in silent wonder and growing admiration for the prophet's obedience and heart for Yahweh, not to mention the straying woman. My gesture in placing my hand upon his shoulder seemed empty or inadequate, but I hoped it conveyed my honor and appreciation. I believe we both sensed the presence of the Qodesh One at that moment.

"But," continued this man whose stature in my heart was growing by the moment, "he had called me to love this woman, the woman G'mer (whose name to you who read, means Completion, for even in and through the straying, he intends to fulfil his purposes). Yahweh had me pursue my wife and redeem her, and name and care for these children whom she bore. And then a third child was to have the most telling name; a son, I was to call him,

9. Israel means Prevailing with God

10. Lo-Ruchamah means No Pity

Lo'Ammiy,[11] for Yahweh was now distancing himself from us—like a statement of divorce because of our straying and sinful ways.

"Oh, what is to be done for these people he created for himself? Upon whom he has lavished such special attention and khesed for such high and distinctive purpose? He wanted me to tell them they are forfeiting their privileged position as his priest among the nations![12] 'Not *my* people', he said, as though to say, 'they look nothing like me'! I can tell you it came as a great shock to me and to The People as well. I'm afraid they had become smug in their privileged position, completely forgetting the responsibility attaching to that privilege. I find it difficult not to become angry and ashamed at their behavior. We are no better than our father 'Dam in Edhen when he forsook his responsibility and forfeited his position! Truly the heart of man is wicked and arrogant! And yet, my dear Ysha'yah, even despite this terrible indictment, do you know what he then told me?"

I looked quizzically at him.

"He said this: 'yet even in the place where it was said lo-am-miy, you are not my people—even there they will again be called, wait for it . . . benei ha Elohim!'"[13]

I was transfixed as I listened, and saw the similarity of the words Yahweh had given us for The People of both the north and south. I was about to break in and speak of the similarities of our experiences, when Hosheah continued. I could see that it was good for him to share his burden with a kindred spirit. The sun had moved and the shade of a large terebinth behind the wall now began to engulf us, so I beckoned in the direction of the Bayth-El and we emerged into the brightness of the sunshine. As we moved we frightened several sparrows that had been feeding on crumbs left by children and, with a whirr of brown-grey wings that adjourned to the dense foliage of the lower branches of the terebinth. Before resuming his theme, Hosheah gasped as

11. Lo-ammiy means Not my People
12. Hosea 4:6b NKJV
13. Hosea 1:10

he caught a first glimpse of the Bayth-El that the great Shalomoh
had built to the glory of Yahweh . . .

"Our task has so often been a thankless one as we have tried
to call the people back from their waywardness; to warn of peril
and to hold up the plumb line of Yahweh's right order by which
a people become great! Why, time without number he has shown
his hand in merciful kindness; time without number he has heard
and healed the land or protected from those who would destroy
us, or blessed us with an abundance that we did not deserve! This
very Bayth-El of Shalomoh is testimony to his beneficence. Why
can the people not feel it also, for it is a heart of blessing and favor.
Persistently hearts have drifted into carelessness and then to enter-
taining other gods which have no reality or existence, save in the
foolish minds of those who fashion them."

As Hosheah spoke I remembered that, as seers, we have observed the poison within the heart of the benei adam, yes and
even in the hearts of those called benei ha Elohim. It is a poison so
difficult to bleed from the veins of the people (for that is where it
seems to reside); a poison that soothes and lulls and de-sensitizes
the mind to mortal dangers. How soon it brings myopia and veils
the very eyes that have beheld wonders from his hand! A poison that seems to invade from birth and against which there is
a simple antidote, for the poison is soon eradicated by practised
love for Yahweh's Law-word, and obedience to it. We have witnessed it again and again within our own lives and in the lives
of all the devout among us who are committed to live as benei
ha Elohim. These are the ones who find that he never fails! Our
task as the seers of Yahweh has been to see what he sees and to
bring his heart to The People. Of course, this frequently means
a division. Sometimes we wish that the great Yahweh Elohim
would just speak with his own voice from the heavens, but we
are reminded that even at Siynay, the Mountain of Elohim, when
Moshe received Torah, all the people heard the voice of Yahweh-
Elohim[14] and yet went off and made a calf! So—he has chosen to
call us as his mouthpiece. It is the way he chooses.

14. Deuteronomy 5:22

CHAPTER 17

Dusk and the coming Dawn

*Then the remnant of Jacob shall be
in the midst of many peoples,
like dew from the LORD,
like showers on the grass,
that tarry for no man nor wait for
the **sons of men** (benei adam)*

(Micah 5:7 NKJV **emphasis**
and parenthesis added)

AND THE TIME CAME. For when Yahweh has spoken, events are set
in train that are irrevocable unless revoked by him. The speaking
establishes the object or the event just as his telling forth established the heavens and the earth and the dwellers upon it. What
he has said is the unstoppable force which can meet no immovable
object. The word travels out through time and space and through
the quantum realms faster than light, creating what has been spoken, whether as substance or as event, causing reality, making it, as
your record so often says, 'come to pass.' And, so it was, that both
the northern portion of Ysra-El, the dwellers in Shomoron and
then later the southern portion of Yudah with their glorious capi-
tal Yerushalem, fell to the goyim just as the prophets had warned.
To the goyim! The benei adam! Those to whom The People had
been called as purveyors of the glory of Yahweh and Adonai. And
now, as we near the end of one system—the one which I know has
been superseded—or better, completed and complemented—I will
bring that great prophet Z'kharyah forward to speak . . .

"Ah yes, I am another of those called to see and to say as Yahweh sees and says. And so, they call us seers and I am the one, Z'kharyah, called by him for the critical time of restoration and rebuilding in Yudah—and especially the rebuilding of our temple, at The Place! And I have seen his heart and I have seen that even after the treatment we accorded him with our straying and fruitless ways, yet he will not let us go. He, unlike us, takes his covenant seriously and without abatement, desires us to be The People who manifest him to all peoples—and in such a way that they are without excuse! And yes, in manifesting him, it's not only his kindness that the nations are to see, but also his severity and how seriously he takes both his covenant and the welfare of The People. Oh, not only do I see his heart, but I see my own and that of The People. It causes me pain.

The coming King!

"But, everlasting praise be to him for he has given me visions and understandings that disclose his unrelenting desire for The People to become everything they can be. I have seen from the visions that he, though sometimes hidden from view, governs all things . . . the nations, kings, armies and events. They all are his. They are all under his command! So, we are seeing the great House rebuilt and the calling back of The People, the benei ha Elohim, to worship and exalt him and, even yet, show his power and truth among the goyim. But, I see also, that all these things speak of something deeper and more real—and yet to come! For I, like others, see the bringing forth of the One known as The Branch, who builds the true temple of Yahweh;[1] and I see a High Priest known as Yeshua and I see a Priest-King coming who rides a donkey, and bringing with him that for which we all long; salvation—salvation for the nations! Oh, it is glorious. I see too, as others of my calling have seen, a fountain opening for cleansing from impurity[2] and—a

1. Zechariah 6:12 & 13
2. Zechariah 13:1

stream of living water, flowing from The Place.[3] The time is near. I see these things as things seen through mist that sometimes lifts and sometimes closes in; what the entire meaning is, I cannot fully see, yet I know as I know nothing else, that he has spoken and I am persuaded of one clear thing: The King is coming, The King is coming.[4] And—he brings salvation for all who will receive him!

3. Zechariah 14:8
4. Zechariah 14:9

Part Five: **New Day!**

CHAPTER 18

Arrival!

I TOLD YOU THERE was a culmination coming. Although we can enter your realm, nonetheless, concerning some matters relating to earth and time creatures, there is for us, a cloud or veil. So, although for Ha Elohim, time events are eternally determined and always seen, for us they are seen only as he allows. It is so with what has unfolded in your realm as an outstanding time event—as it turns out—*the* most significant event of all your time events! For it is nothing less than a Parousia; the arrival of him as one of you, on earth. Perhaps this is easier for you, who know the thing called sin and the thing called faith, to understand. Yet, what we perceive is that many of your kind are indifferent to this, the signal event of your journey in time, as though it did not matter!

Let me enlarge on what I just said about this being a time event. Whilst that is so, it is really an event determined from his realm, eternity. It has been determined and extant since *before* time! Your own apostle Yohannes has come close to expressing it when he wrote that Iesous Christos is 'the lamb slain from the foundation of the world.'[1] But for you, it had to occur somewhere along the line you call time. It has then, a before and an after; a prelude and a postlude! Insofar as we can place ourselves inside your framework we can view it from your perspective. Can you see now, that what is called the Old Testament describes the period in which humans were always being pointed forward to *the* event whilst the New points those who live after it, back to it? And—that

1. Revelation 13:8 NKJV

the pointing is always the task of those known as the sons of God (in the language of the Old, the benei ha Elohim; in that of the New, uioi theou or tekna theou). They have been chosen to be always pointing to him!

The Segue

We see that many in your day seem to make far too much of the difference between the two, that is, what you have called the Old and the New. For in the view of Yahweh they are simply two parts of a whole—all of a piece. It is merely the fact that for you, the *arrival*, the act of becoming-one-of-you, necessarily had to occur at a particular moment along the line. For you who read, the arrival occurred something a little over two thousand of your years, in your past. You are pointed back to it, but that moment was simply the start of his bringing into their fullest expression and meaning all the previous special feasts and celebrations of the benei ha Elohim! It's true, one is the Old and it is followed by the New, but they are much more a unity than many in your day consider. For they are complementary in the sense that the New brings to fruition the Old, whilst the Old is the indispensable foundation upon which the New finds rest! The One who arrived *became* (and *is*), you see, the consummation of Chag HaMotzi, ha Pesakh and of Shabbat—and then of Shavu'ot; and in a while, the denouement of Yom Teru'ah! It's *all* entailed in *him*—the past, the present and what is yet to come; they all mean *him* and all find their meaning completed in him and his work! And that is why he chose certain men such as Saul of Tarsus (who became Paul), who was a Rabbi steeped in the Hebrew truth and traditions. It is why Iesous was born a Jew, in the great lineage of Abraham and David for the story (indeed *his*-story) is that of how those known as sons of God continue through all of time until the end. There was to be a segue at a point in time, into the fulfillments; into recognition that all was now met; all the Law, all the feasts, all the offerings, all the requirements for righteousness—all met, in *him*! For all mankind!

I, and those of my kind are seeing the purpose of his long-anticipated arrival in your world and it is extraordinary almost beyond your words to describe. For at an appointed and exactly right moment of your time,[2] the One in whom all the meaning resides, took your flesh and became one of you—oh, it is so mysterious to us who observe. For we know what was relinquished, so that this could become reality! We have seen the limitations and constraints of time—and wonder how you dwell there! Yet here is what we see and know; that he has willingly become less than us to become one of you. Then, among you, he has done something that we could never have dreamed possible! He has become a benei adam—or in the language of the era and people among whom he did it, huios anthropou—son of man! *The* Son of Man! It was done through a woman's womb in a creative work of Elohim Holy Spirit! It is a wonder on the same level as that which we beheld at your beginnings when he fashioned 'Dam from dust and breathed his own life-breath into him. And he came to you from the long-prepared lineage of the benei ha Elohim.

The veil has not lifted fully for us concerning his purpose in this, and yet we perceive that it clearly has to do with what he and you call sin. We have seen that there had been a veil of darkness separating you from him and which could not be penetrated from your side. Yet, it appears to us that he has suddenly pierced it—yes, and from your side, for that is where he was, opening a door that was shut—indeed, making a door where none existed; a door and a communion between you and his Father for those who will use it. It is a marvel! It required of him that thing you call death and yet we see that his dying is somehow a representative death into which you are all invited, so that you may then enter something greater—a shared life with him—both in your time realm and then beyond it! For he, as a prototype, was brought back from (and through) that thing! The thing that secured every other creature without escape through all your history, has suddenly been, by his conquest of it, rendered ineffective! It once had power; it has it no more! What is this? For we now see some of

2. Romans 5:6

your kind who experience death, move through it, straight into our realm, as though it didn't even exist now! They die and yet are, at the same moment, in his presence even while what remains of them returns to your earth. We know now, with the partial lifting of the veil that limits our understanding, that the actual person of your kind exists separately to the visible, material shell in which it is housed! This is a discovery to us. You too, are of the spirit realm, but you have been given a house of flesh for your dwelling in time. It is your carriage to transport you through your time journey; a journey which concludes when the carriage is discarded. Actually, one thing he has made us aware of is this; that time itself (at least as you know and experience it) will be discarded too! Yes—this may come as a shock to some of you, but time is just a construct for a specially created order of beings—for which he has a special and particular purpose.

But yes, to return to my track—he arrived, as one of you, and here's the point: it was the denouement of the fresh start for your entire kind—the new day hinted at and often spoken of by the prophets among the benei ha Elohim. This arrival had begun all the way back; he had spoken it and spoken it and at last the word became flesh! Yes, even as one of your writers has expressed it, he materialized as the new and second Adam[3] for the entirely new creation he had been telling you about for ages![4] He began his first creation with the heavens and your earth and finished it with you. However, this new creation is in the reverse order, beginning with you and being completed with a new heaven and a new earth![5] This was news to us, but some of your own, those called Apostles with whom he spent his earth time, have written of it. And now—let me tell you the outcome of this 'arrival' among you, for we have watched in awe and wonder—as we have, of all the things he accomplishes. But oh! We see the close, the special . . . how shall I describe it? The *joined-with-him* place that you earthlings enjoy as beings made, if you please, *in his image and likeness!*

3. 1 Corinthians 15:45–49
4. See for example, 2 Corinthians 5:17
5. 2 Peter 3:13

CHAPTER 19

The new People sing and dance again!

*Behold what manner of love . . . . that we should be called the **sons of God** (tekna theou)* (1 John 3:1 KJV **emphasis** and parenthesis added)

*But you are a chosen generation, a royal priesthood, a holy nation, His own special people, that you may proclaim the praises of Him who called you out of darkness into His marvelous light; who once were not a people but are now **the people** of God, who had not obtained mercy but now have obtained mercy'.* (1 Peter 2:9 & 10 NKJV **emphasis** added)

I SHAQAAD, HAVE TRIED to help you see the journey. Mind you, there's a sense in which you should see it more clearly than us, but we do have the advantage of being above and beyond your time sphere. For us, it's much like your experience of looking at a map. I imagine that when you are at street level in an unknown city, all can be somewhat confusing if you're trying to find your way. Your maps give you what is more like our view, a sky view.

My objective in our short period together, has been to help you to see what we see, and particularly, how there have always been two streams flowing through your history. One is the stream of humans who follow the inner pull that he puts within every one of you. We see that he ensures that any who begin genuinely to pursue that, are led to more and more light! We've watched and wondered at his grace in this. The stream that chooses him becomes to him, his sons—the sons of God (as was his original intention—a family known by his name), whilst those who walk their own way remain but sons of men. Now, what I must point out to you is that those who wrote down the story of his arrival and the introduction of his better covenant, continued to use the same figures of speech.

But first, a few other important things; things that make your history hang together. For when he came among you, it was to accomplish something of eternal consequence almost beyond comprehension to us. As I have said, this thing called sin (which was nothing more nor less than your choosing to walk in your own way, rather than to follow his voice within) was the cause of the veil of darkness between you and he. And, as I've also mentioned, (and at the risk of repetition for we feel this needs emphasis) it was he who punched a hole right through that darkness! But, how he did this, I want to try to further explain. It was the event that enables you to move through that hole, into a new dimension of living. When any one of you does so, you move from being a son (or child) of man only, to being a new kind of creature—huios theou—a son of God!

Restart!

Here is how it appears to us—and I can only hope it is helpful in some way. Get ready for this, for it is a marvel—and yet shows how he can make a way when there is none apparent! He became one of you! That's right, a son of man; another, or a new, Adam; but he didn't do what the first Adam did. Though he arrived, as has been written, 'in the *likeness* of sinful flesh,'[1] he didn't sin; never gave way to darkness! To us, what this appears to mean is that where Adam number one failed, *he* did not! It was a completely new start for you, with Yahweh himself taking on the role, arriving on the human stage to provide a new way! He was even tested, as was the first Adam, but didn't slip, but . . . and here is where the mystery really takes hold; just as Adam had been banished from the garden

1. Paul in Romans 8:3

and from access to the tree of life, this last Adam too, suffered a banishment, even though he hadn't sinned! We can only explain this as him, somehow, taking upon himself—for every one of you—the banishment from the presence of Elohim that is always the inevitable result of walking independently. And this appears to have been accomplished in a physical death in which he bore away, as your representative, the banishment consequence of all your independence! The banishment of the first Adam excluded him and he could not, by himself, make a way back. But this Adam number two, made a way back. I told you it was a mystery! What this now seems to mean is that you are no longer separated, unless you, for some very foolish reason, choose to be! All the things that were introduced into earth's equations when the first Adam went independent, seem miraculously to have been recovered by the obedience of this new One! The dark barrier between you and the Father has been removed. Gone! the way back to the other tree—the one called 'Life,' has been restored. Indeed, this One who arrived among you, the shoot from the root of Jesse, is himself, the new Tree of Life, And . . . the thing called Death: why—it has been, it seems to us—annihilated; yes, killed off! How have we seen this? We saw as we watched; the thing which had held every one of you since the first Adam, in its thrall, has now, mysteriously, no power at all. None. For he went right through it and out the other side— yes, to our side where there is no such thing!

But, hear this, for this is the part that causes us to magnify him more than ever for the working of his power. Nothing seems impossible to him. For here is what we have observed; that those who will receive the thing he holds out to you, called faith—yes, those who are given this and take it, he then takes with him, right through that most-feared thing! Through it, I say and clean out the other side, into our realm where, we have seen dimly, you are later to receive a new 'carriage'; this time, one untrammeled by the faults and limits of your independence-spoiled, earth-life. And we have only learned this by looking over the shoulders (to use one of your sayings) of those apostles, who have been treated to glimpses of things we have not! You—and I mean the new sons—are to be elevated to a station somewhere above our own. In fact, to become virtually, (and, I think, actually), one with him as a wife to her husband! But we are glad, and dance with him and with you in this for we know that with him, none of us is ever impoverished. He does everything for the betterment of every one of his creatures. We are in awe. These, as I say, are things we understand from those among you to whom he has shown them.

Ah, but there is more. For I must tell you what I have seen about those now called huioi theou, yes, sons of God, as distinct from those called huioi anthropoi. For I have seen that these descriptions for the two streams of humans has carried all the way through your time's span. I will show you how those who set down the record of his coming among you, and those he commissioned to instruct you, carried the idea forward in what you have called the new covenant. It is a good name, for it describes it exactly. All his operations among you through time have been on the foundation of covenant promise, just as it is in your current situation.

CHAPTER 20

Authority to become sons

HERE IT IS AGAIN. That thing . . . the gift he gives, that you call faith. I, Shaqaad and all of us have witnessed its role in his relationship with you. For it appears there is no other way. It is by it that you receive the new life, his life; for that is what happens. An exchange takes place—his life for yours, but there must be a relinquishing of yours for this to occur! And that is the transaction that accompanies the gift called faith; a sometimes ready, sometimes almost reluctant giving up of self in order to receive what's on offer. For some, it is quite a struggle, after which they wonder why! But it is always by faith as one of your own has written, 'to as many as received him, believing on his name, to them he gave authority to become sons of God.'[1] Of course, to us, yet again, we are entering the realm of mystery, but what we do see is the change that takes place in this transaction; oh yes, we see it! You become the new thing upon relinquishing the old; in fact, the old fades away and a newly given authority carries you forward.[2] And, the old from which you are changed, is that tragic likeness to all the other sons of men. That's why we see the change. It's a metamorphosis. From one form to another; sons of men to sons of God. It's from darkness to light; veiled to un-veiled; from futility to purpose. From death to life! That's how visible it is—and, it's not just us who see this. To others of your kind too, it is usually quite visible and clear. But it is always this becoming new 'sons' or, if you prefer, 'children,'

1. John 1:12
2. 2 Corinthians 5:17

but what is being conveyed is the truth of you becoming inheritors, together with him! Yes, inheritors in his kingdom of all that has been entrusted to him by the Father.

But, I must bring forward your apostles with words, inspired by him, and which highlight the same idea carried right through your scriptures. We ask your attention, as the one called Paulos speaks . . .

"Yes, yes, O Watcher Shaqaad, for I had seen from the old writings (in which I was very well educated) that those who were in the stream that departed from him, were called from of old, benei adam—sons of men; and our Lord used the same term. I remember our dear brother Marcus speaking of it when we journeyed together. He told me that when Iesous Christos spoke to those who accused him of driving out demons by Beelzebub, he reprimanded them and said that all manner of blasphemies among the sons of men (huioi anthropoi) could be forgiven, except for that kind, against his dear Spirit![3] Because I was so familiar with the scriptures of the other covenant, I recognized the description immediately. Indeed, I believe I used it myself often, as for example, when I wrote to my friends in the church at Ephesow. I wrote about the mystery now revealed—that the gospel has now made the ethnoi (Gentiles) sons and heirs as well! I pointed out that this had not been made known to the sons of men in previous generations, but is now made evident![4] And that other term used in the old, benei ha Elohim, why, I most certainly carried that into the new revelation! I made use of it in our language as huiois, (or tekna) Theou (sons of God) time and again as did Iesous Christos[5] himself and most of our writers such as Yohannes and Lucas.[6] Yes, all who know him have moved from one condition to the other. It is a thing worthy of our everlasting praise, that he became like a

3. Mark 3:28–29

4. Ephesians 3:5–6

5. Matthew 5:9, 44–45

6. See for example, Luke 6:35; John 1:12–13; also, Romans 8:14, 16, 21; Romans 9:8; 2 Corinthians 6:18; Galatians 3:26; 4:1–8; Ephesians 1:5; 1 John 3:3:1–3

son of man so that we might become sons of God—or, let me put it another way—that *the* Son of Man came to bear away all our shortcomings, so that we all may become sons of God."

So, my dear reader, you see things that, though clouded to us the Watchers, nonetheless bring great honor to him. We see that though you have, each one of you, followed your own hearts in the ways of the sons of men, he would not let you escape his relentless love and his plan for you. He has, as only he could, made a way back where none existed. A way, *the* way— for you to be received again as sons, and more, much more, than sons—as heirs! And now I speak of things I do know a little about for I see this side. Your world is indeed full of beauty, though tarnished by the thing known as darkness; but that beauty is not to be compared with that of this side; it is not able to be made into words, such is the expanse, the limitlessness, the ever-ness and unfolding vibrancy of what is here! I know that some of you—like Paulos who has just shared with you—have seen glimpses of it. But it is so distant from your unaided and earth-bound comprehension, that even he with his gift to describe things spiritual, has been curtailed from sharing its wonders.[7] You must await the new day, when as sons of God, you leave behind the constraints of your feeble carriage, or are gathered from your earth, that temporary construct made for temporary purposes, to enter this realm, exalted to a place of higher rank than ours!

7. 2 Corinthians 12:2–4

CHAPTER 21

The song continues: many sons to glory!

. . . they sang a new song, saying: *"You are worthy to take the scroll, and to open its seals; For You were slain, and have redeemed us to God by your blood out of every tribe and tongue and people and nation, and have made us kings and priests to our God; and we shall reign on the earth.* (Revelation 5:9–10 NKJV **emphasis** added)

. . . but while he was yet afar off, his father saw him, and was moved with compassion, and ran, and fell on his neck, and kissed him . . . (and) the father said to his servants, "Bring forth quickly the best robe, and put it on him; and put a ring on his hand, and shoes on his feet: and bring the fatted calf, and kill it, and let us eat, and make merry: for this my son *was dead, and is alive again; he was lost, and is found"* (Luke 15:20–23 NKJV excerpts **emphasis** added)

*For the anxious longing of the creation waits eagerly for the revealing of the **sons of God** . . . .because the creation itself also will be delivered from the bondage of corruption into the glorious liberty of the **children of God*** (Romans 8:19 NASV **emphasis** added)

*For it was fitting for Him, for whom are all things and by whom are all things, in bringing **many sons to glory**, to make the captain of their salvation perfect through sufferings* (Hebrews 2:10 NKJV **emphasis** added)

I, SHAQAAD AND OTHER Watchers were privileged to hear the extraordinary song at what you call the Beginning. It was the music of our realm, in yours. Indescribable harmonies of color and sound; pro-creative, infusing, dancing among and through the spheres faster than light, more generous and engulfing than universes, adding vibrancy, sustaining and validating everything touched. Indeed, as we have said, becoming symphonic as all things in that beginning of the earth and time realm, began to be fruitful. As our sojourn together is concluding, let me take you back there momentarily dear reader. Remember how I described it to you? All things sang together in this 'other-worldly' song, as the fecundity of our realm was introduced by the miracle of Creator, into this new place;[1] a place and a cosmos which, strangely, had the appearance of substance. We could see that it was a construct. A construct of particles and light, brought to temporary solidity to the sight and touch of its newly-created beings who were made, if you please, in the very likeness of their Creator. Made with something of him, within each one; an *I am* as a reflection of his great *I AM*! We knew that there was nothing else in all creation like this, or like them—these extraordinary image–of–Elohim beings. We knew—or at least had inklings of, the truth that your home was a temporary construct. Indeed, almost a phantasm—like what you call in your day, a hologram—and that you were really spirit beings as us, except that the individual 'you', the 'I am' that comprised every one of you, was housed within a shell, or rather, a carriage. The carriage as I have said, was to bear you along in your works of pro-creativity with him! This, we had never seen before. It was clear that with you, he had done something new and unique. But, to return to the music, the song and the symphony: it was the sound of productivity and joy and all was ascribed to, and found its home with . . . him. It became, as it were, the Throne upon which he was enthroned as it continually acknowledged him as the One from whom all flowed and for

---

1. Job 38:7. Note '*all* the sons of God sang': in the author's view this means those 'sons' (created beings) of both the heavenly and the earthly realm; NKJV emphasis added.

113

whose purpose it existed! But the song and symphony came to an abrupt halt, after which there arose only occasional discordant sounds. And now? Why, we see and hear that the song has been resumed . . . is being resumed and growing in strength! Yes, in a new creation! This time however, the fruit is within human lives and spilling out of them to draw others into the choir and its new song. And it's happening all over your world, among every type of your kind, as he seems to be making a new people to one day inhabit a totally new world. Your own writers have said, 'a new heaven and a new earth, wherein right order dwells.'[2] Sounds exciting to us. We love all his creative acts and works.

Once more—The People

Once more, I Shaqaad am indebted to that apostle Petros, whom we see, took up the idea that Yahweh brought through Prophet Hosheah in a different time and age. For Petros has seen by the breathing of Yahweh's Spirit, that The People continue to exist in your present age. He has quoted Hosheah thus—

> 'But you are a chosen generation,
> a royal priesthood, a holy nation,
> His own special people,
> that you may proclaim the praises
> of Him who called you out of darkness
> into His marvelous light; who once were
> not a people but are now *the people*
> of God, who had not obtained mercy
> but now have obtained mercy'[3]

Petros has used all the same words to describe the sons of God in your age as were used in Hosheah's; chosen, holy, special, The People! And all for a purpose—to proclaim his praises. You see, it's just as it was then. The world of the sons of men is in darkness. A light must be seen. Light is always evident in contrast to

2. 2 Peter 3:13
3. 1 Peter 2:9,10

darkness and any among the sons of men may come to it and into it—if they choose.

We see too, that he 'hymns' with you in your song to God, for it has been written that he is among you in the congregation, joining in with you![4] Yes, it is right where the writer reminds you that when you are sons, you are of the same family—and he means of the one Father![5] He has made you all sons and brothers, or, if you prefer, children, alongside him who is your Elder Brother!

But now, let me take you to what you call the end, for it is a majestic conclusion! I have seen it; again, only by looking over the shoulder of that apostle of yours known as Yohannes, who was given a remarkable un-veiling.[6] He received an invitation, 'Come up here, and I will show you what must take place after this', at which he was ushered into the Throne Room from which to view your history as though from various windows![7] As I've said, we have not the view that he was given, but we see that it was indeed, an amazing revealing. There is far too much there to discuss, but here is what we do see. Its entire message is about those who overcome. Yes, Yohannes has used that word many times[8] in his writing of the un-veiling; it is the major theme. But, here is what I wanted to tell you. At the end, Yohannes sees the culmination and hears the One who is described as Alpha and Omega, speak of the fountain of living water of life that he gives without cost to everyone who is thirsty![9] And then this . . . 'he who overcomes (nikeo) shall *inherit* all things, and I will be his God and *he shall be my son.*'[10] Aha! The thing he has always desired; sons and heirs, who have become joint-heirs with his eternally begotten son! He who *overcomes* shall

---

4. Hebrews 2:12 where the Greek word is humneo, to hymn, to celebrate

5. Hebrews 2:11. See ASV and various translations 'all of one' meaning of the same Source or Father

6. In Revelation 1:1, apokalupsis means uncovering, revealing

7. See this author's book, 'Windows on a World gone Wrong.'

8. The Greek verb to overcome, nikeo or derivations of it is used some 15 times in The Revelation

9. Revelation 21:6

10. Revelation 21:7

be his son! Now, as seen by us, this is a marvel of grace! For we have seen the separating darkness; and have seen that it is all his work to tear it away so that you could again, become sons. As always—as it has ever been through your earth history—there is overcoming to be done if you are to be his sons. Before you make the choice to become sons, the darkness owns you. You are, in fact, sons of men and sons of their darkness, for that is where they live, without him; in the dark. Oh, and Yohannes continues, to describe them—those who choose not to be his sons—as, wait for it—cowardly and unbelieving; and worse! We are saddened that some of you, after all that he has done to redeem you and bring you back into sonship, could be so foolish and hard of heart as to reject such a grace; such an overture! 'He shall be my son'! What a glorious and, we would expect, precious–beyond–price, thing for you humans as Yohannes said elsewhere, 'behold; of what kind is this love that Father has bestowed on us, that we become named, *sons of God*'![11] There it is; the intention of the Father, as has been so beautifully rendered in the writings, to bring many sons to glory![12] To do so required that he send a champion as one of you, to be *the* Overcomer to redeem the way that was lost through Adam.

And now dear reader, it is time to conclude, with the hope that you who read—if not yet, will soon be among those known as the sons of God. I have tried to help you see that the platform for the whole journey is really an artifice. It is his invention. If you should ask 'why?', the best answer I can give is, because he could, and he did! Because you were his heart's desire. A new order of being, dwelling in a temporal and temporary construct; a cosmos having a beginning and an end, a reflection of his realm and dwelling–place; with new creatures, with god–likeness, to eternally inhabit, fill, and bring it to similarity to his.

We have come full circle. Your time realm and span are so intrinsically entailed with him who describes himself as Alpha and Omega, Beginning and End, First and Last,[13] that it seems

11. 1 John 3:1 Scripture4all and Author's translation

12. Hebrews 2:10

13. Revelation 22:13 (see also 1:8 and 21:6)

impossible to separate them. Paulos has so well written, 'for he is before all things and by him all things are held together.'[14] He has inserted himself into the web and fabric of your temporal cosmos in a way that is unmistakable and sublime. It may look to you like an experiment, but we believe not. We have seen so many of his works. No, it is overflowing with intention and grace. The creature failed; become a disappointment, but only so that a greater mercy might be revealed, the calling out of a people, The People who love him by choice and choose to become again, eternal, through his gift of eternal life. The construct, the artifice will be dissolved. . .at what you call the end. There will be no further need for it. For at the end, he will have redeemed for himself, The People, as well as his lost creation. The old creation, as we have said, began with the heavens and the earth and concluded with man; the new reverses the order. We see that it begins with man and concludes with the new heaven and the new earth. The platform, the construct, will be discarded and he will make, if you please, a new heaven and a new earth for . . . The People! The plan to have beings, made eternal, occupying and governing a colony of heaven will have been fulfilled. We see that he said it this way. . .'Look, the dwelling-place of God is with men. He will dwell with them and they shall be *His People*. God himself will be with them and will wipe every tear from their eyes, and there will be no more death or sorrow or crying or pain. All these things are gone forever.'[15]

Fare well human companion! I have enjoyed our sojourn. You were made for eternity and eternity for you. Choose life; choose the gift; choose sonship that you too may say with all prodigals who've come home, "Beloved, now are we the *sons of God*, and it does not yet appear what we shall be: but we know that, when he shall appear, we shall be like him; for we shall see him as he is."[16]

---

14. Colossians 1:17

15. Revelation 21:4 Scripture4all and author's translation (*emphasis added*)

16. 1 John 3:2 AKJV (*emphasis added*)

www.ingramcontent.com/pod-product-compliance
Lightning Source LLC
Chambersburg PA
CBHW060403090426
42734CB00011B/2250